Charles Connolly, editor

ON BEING CATHOLICS

FOUR COURTS PRESS • DUBLIN
LUMEN CHRISTI PRESS • HOUSTON

This book was typeset in IBM Baskerville 11 on 12 pt
by Vermilion, Clondalkin, Co. Dublin.

Nihil obstat: Stephen J. Greene, censor deputatus.
Imprimi potest: Dermot Archbishop of Dublin,
31 May 1983. The Nihil obstat and Imprimi potest
are a declaration that a book or publication is con-
sidered to be free from doctrinal or moral error. This
declaration does not imply approval of, or agreement
with, the contents, opinions or statements expressed.

ISBN 0-906127-66-1 cased Four Courts edition
ISBN 0-906127-65-3 paperback Fourt Courts edition
ISBN 0-912414-37-5 Lumen Christi edition

Published by Fourt Courts Press Limited,
Kill Lane, Blackrock, Co. Dublin, Ireland.
and Lumen Christi Press, P.O. Box 13176,
Pech Road, Houston, Texas 77055.

Printed in Ireland.

ACKNOWLEDGEMENTS

The contribution 'The Blessed Eucharist' is
based on the article first published in **Position
Paper 65** (Dublin, May 1979); the essay by
Pedro Rodriguez was first published in two
parts in **Position Paper 85** (January 1981) and
Position Paper 97 (January 1982).

First impression September 1983
Second impression September 1983

CONTENTS

CONTRIBUTORS

Fr Charles Connolly BA, PhD is co-editor of *Position Papers,* Dublin.

Michael Adams is publisher at Irish Academic Press, Dublin.

Pedro Rodriguez is professor of dogmatic theology at the University of Navarre, editor of *Scripta Theologica* and a member of the Pontifical Roman Academy of Saint Thomas.

Eamon Sweeney BE, MEngSc, DD is chaplain to Nullamore University Residence, Dublin.

Introduction

Charles Connolly

When some time ago Michael Adams handed me a manuscript and asked for my opinion I couldn't but have a certain tingling feeling of anticipated excitement. In one of his early contributions to *Position Papers* he said of himself 'I'm a *Catcher in the Rye* man myself.' I didn't understand then what he meant, but in the matter of 'scandalous' religious writing 'I'm an Adams man myself'.

Accordingly I looked forward to an enjoyable hour or two reading his latest salvo. Nor was I disappointed.

He argues, to a lapsed Catholic, that if someone wants to take issue with the Church, then let it be on serious grounds, let it be for 'the right reasons'. He identifies these grounds as Church teaching on the Eucharist, the infallibility of the Pope, and the position of Mary.

What he said struck a chord in me immediately, reminding me of two phrases I had heard often from the lips of the Founder of Opus Dei: 'Omnes cum Petro ad Iesum per Mariam' — All with Peter to Jesus through Mary' *(The Way,* No. 833). And again: 'Christ, Mary, the Pope. Have we not just indicated, in these three words, the loves which sum up the Catholic faith?'

If Christianity is about love, and it is, it is about love of the Father and of the Son and of the Holy Spirit; a love which springs from knowledge through faith and is expressed in deeds and service. It is also about love of the Incarnate Word, Jesus Christ our Saviour; of Mary his Mother and our Mother, type of the Church, from the first moment of her earthly life — the Immaculate Conception — to the last — her glorious Assumption into heaven; and of Peter and his successors, bishops of Rome and bishops of the Catholic Church.

After putting down the manuscript and thinking: yes, this should be published because it may just shock someone enough to make him or her react, I had second thoughts. That wouldn't be sufficient. Sustained commitment, action and effort need to be

7

built on a solid basis of sound doctrinal instruction. We need to know and be able to explain what we believe; otherwise our faith is in danger of being undermined. So, it was decided to expand the project into a full book, including three articles which would develop each of the three 'scandals' dealt with.

It is natural enough to want to speak and write of the Eucharistic Sacrifice because it is the centre and root of our Christian life and has been under question in recent times, as Pope Paul VI pointed out in his encyclical *Mysterium Fidei:*

> We have become aware that there are a number of speakers and writers on this sacred mystery who are propagating opinions that are likely to disturb the minds of the faithful and to cause them considerable mental confusion in matters of faith. Such opinions relate to Masses celebrated privately, to the dogma of transubstantiation and to eucharistic worship. They seem to think that, although a doctrine has been defined once by the Church, it is open to anyone to ignore it or to give it an interpretation that whittles away the natural meaning of the words or the accepted sense of the concepts.

The Pope's infallibility, its scope and nature, had to be explained in detail, because of its importance and because of its relevance in ecumenical dialogue.

It has often been said in the past, and it is as true today as it ever was, that any Church which does not claim to teach and guide with the infallible authority of Jesus could in no way be the *true* Church of Christ. And so, Vatican Council II teaches that 'the sole Church of Christ . . .constituted and organised as a society present in the world, subsists in the Catholic Church, which is governed by the successor of Peter and by the bishops in communion with him' *(Lumen Gentium,* 8) and 'the Catholic Church has been endowed with all divinely revealed truth and with all the means of grace' *Unitatis redintegratio,* 4).

The Pope's infallibility — to be exercised under rigorously defined conditions — is simply an extension of the Church's infallibility, and this in turn is the result of Christ being 'with us until the end of time'.

Our faith in the Eucharist and other teachings of the Church is sustained by the word of Jesus echoing in the Church throughout the centuries.

Our hope is enhanced by seeing in the risen Jesus, and in Mary assumed into heaven, our ultimate destiny. In Mary we have a human person who has travelled the road we must travel, but who has travelled it to the very end. Mary's assumption simply shows us the glorious resurrection in store for all of us if we are faithful and true. 'At his coming all men will rise with their bodies and will be judged according to their deeds. Those who have done well will go into eternal life; those who have done evil will go into eternal fire. This is the Catholic faith. Unless a man believes it faithfully and firmly, he cannot be saved' *(Anthanasian Creed)*.

It is my hope that those who, after reading this book, remain or become Catholics for the right reasons, will be stimulated to study further the teachings of the Church.

On being Catholics for right reasons

Michael Adams

Why is it that these days you meet more and more people who either don't practise their religion or say they no longer believe in it at all? Why is it, you might ask yourself, that *I* am not into religion, that it doesn't mean much to me?

To someone who does practise his religion these are not academic questions, for basically Catholics who do practise and Catholics who don't are made of the same stuff: neither is so bizarre that they can't compare notes. And in some way other people's failure to practise is a failure on the part of those who do. For religion really to work it should not just work for me in my 'private' religious life: it should work in my 'public' religious life also, in my 'apostolate'. I do notice, however, a tendency to say: Well, if he wants to do his own thing, that's his affair. Yet, however much respect Christians have for other people's freedom, it is part and parcel of being a Christian to interfere to some extent in other people's lifes: we are directed to the corporal works of mercy — and to the spiritual works of mercy (which include, for example, counselling the doubtful and instructing the ignorant). Not that our lives have to be spent asking people Christian questions: we have lots of other proper things to do and, besides, with the best will in the world we often do funk the encounter or don't really know how to express our concern in an acceptable way. But we know that we have a right and a duty to be concerned: even our sense of justice tells us this. If I know from my experience that trying to be a good Catholic *is worth while now,* then people who are not moving in that direction are losing out.

Saint Peter advises *us* when he tells the early Christians: 'Always be prepared to make a defence to any one who calls you to account for the hope that is in you, yet do it with gentleness and reverence' (1 Peter 3:15): Christians are meant to be happy people — so happy that others, if they are alert, will want to find out the reason for their joy. His colleague, Paul, is even more vigorous as we can see from this passage: 'For, "every one who calls upon the name of the Lord will be saved". But how are men to call upon him in whom they have not believed? And how are they to believe in him of whom they have never heard? And how are they to hear without a preacher? And how can men preach unless they are sent? As it is written, "How beautiful are the feet of those who preach good news!"... So faith comes from what is heard, and what is heard comes by the preaching of Christ' (Rom 10:13ff). For Christianity to happen, Christ has to be preached: people have to talk to other people about the gospel.

Who are these preachers? The most obvious ones are the bishops and priests of the Church, people with a special mission: that is the orthodox Catholic answer; but the Church also knows that many of the people that you and I meet will rarely come across Christian preachers and if they do there is a good chance that they won't even switch on to what they are saying, never mind act on what they hear (a huge exception to this is the preaching of John Paul II). To a great extent people are awakened to religion — if they are awakened to it at all — by their fellow travellers, the ordinary people, Christians, whom they happen to get to know in the ordinary ways of life. If *we* don't have an answer ready, if we don't say anything to them, they won't get a chance to hear; and if we do say something then perhaps they will be more inclined to listen than if some stranger approaches them 'official-like' or they happen to stop at a street corner to hear an itinerant preacher do his thing: they are most unlikely to stop, because generally they are going somewhere (people are always hurrying) or think they have heard it all before.

You may say: but God has his ways of speaking to the soul. Indeed; but what if God's way is you or I? 'God will provide' preachers; but he *has* provided them; even though we are no great shakes he can use us.

Nor is it enough to say: they can read the Bible. Yes, ignorance of Scripture is ignorance of God; yet lots of people read the Bible and it hasn't made them good Catholics. The Bible, I'm afraid, is not enough; what brings people into religion is *the Church* and what keeps them in it is *the Church* (whether they are aware of this or not is another thing). Most Catholics are into religion because we were brought up in it; and if you have ever read accounts of how adults joined the Church ('conversion stories') you must have noticed that they came by all sorts of routes and that other (ordinary) people played a big part in their conversion. How did they do it? Wittingly and unwittingly, through their friendship, their letters, their writings, their natural charm, shared experiences, emotional involvement, and sexual attraction (how many have entered the Church via marriage?) — and 'good example', which sounds so formal and contrived but usually is not. But in the process of coming to grips with the Catholic religion there is one input which always must be there: *intelligence*. People cannot operate as Catholics without, to some extent, applying their mind to the business. They could become a sort of pentecostal Christians by singing or feeling their way into religion (and we would be silly not to acknowledge the role of passions and emotions) but the Catholic religion does require people to apply their minds. This is not to say that people can think their way into the Church (proud intellectual agnostics, for example, lack the basic humility that faith grows on) but without thinking, without weighing reasons and arriving at conscientious decisions, no adult is going to progress in faith: *Catholic faith is a reasonable service*; however higher, surer, quicker, broader the knowledge that comes via the gift of faith, that knowledge is in continuity, to some degree, with the knowledge that comes from reason.

This — for a Catholic — is no mere matter of opinion. One hundred years ago the Ecumenical Council of Vatican I made dogmatic statements along these lines. At that time it was all the rage to shut religion off into a sort of vague 'spiritual' world unconnected with reason and logic and natural science: religion could be true but you could not prove it was true. Vatican I warned Christians that God is not only the object of faith (a supernatural gift which some people had and some hadn't); he is also the object of reason: the existence of a personal providential God and his main attributes can be known by the light of human reason; moreover, the data of faith can and should be explored by reason, thus creating a Christian philosophy and theology which are scientific; there is no justification for jettisoning reason in order to make a leap into the dark and *then* find the light of God's super-natural revelation. Vatican I's teaching provides Catholics (and everyone who is ready to listen to it) with the ability to face the world of science with assurance, confident that there can be no clash between knowledge acquired by reason ('science') and knowledge acquired by faith. Indeed you could say that this teaching was the immediate basis for Vatican II's confident approach to the world of our own time; without it, there would have been no point in trying to promote any sort of meaningful conversation between Christians (the Church) and other people (the 'world' as yet unchristianised): the language of either would be gibberish to the other.

The net result of all this is that as far as Catholics are concerned there is always and everywhere scope for some sort of apologia for the faith, some 'apologetics', some intellectual discussion aimed at 'explaining the reason for our hope'. Arguments? Not arguments in the sense of trying to clobber people in conversation or in books; but, yes, arguments in the sense of explaining what truths of faith mean (pushing back the frontier of mystery, which is indeed at the core of religion) and showing why it makes sense to practise the Catholic faith: without theological action of this type (at all sorts of intellectual levels) the Catholic faith cannot be passed on.

This apologia — contained in any proper apostolate — is not just a hook for landing the fish, for attracting non-believers; it is also a factor in helping Catholics themselves to practise their religion or to continue to be faithful. *Perhaps*, if we were very docile (mentally and spiritually), we would not give a thought to the reasons behind, for example, *Humanae Vitae*; but most of us want to know not just what is the teaching of the Church; the why of the teaching is also important: it helps to feel that not only are we being *faithful* when we are trying to be good Catholics but we are being *reasonable* when we are fighting the good fight: our religion makes human sense, our faith is a reasonable service. Indeed, in the practice of religion God expects us to use our human resources, our natural grace/endowment (e.g. reason and natural virtue and will-power) as well as supernatural grace (the additional gifts he gives so we can know his inner personality and grow in intimacy with him).

IF I WERE GOING TO TRY TO FOCUS SOMEONE'S MIND ON THE CATHOLIC RELIGION, IS THERE ANY SUCH THING AS A SHORT CUT?

I recently had a short conversation on the road with a German art student from Frankfurt: a pleasant fellow, baptised a Catholic, non-practising, intelligent, *au fait* with contemporary philosophy, apparently not vicious, interested in finding answers to the big questions. What could you usefully say to him in half an hour?

His difficulty seemed to be that he regarded the Church as an institution and therefore something always out of date and out of touch with modernity; also, he (or perhaps it was someone else) said that the Church's rules, especially moral rules, were too hard. His name is Ino, and there are lots of Inos around: some of them make the very same points, and the rest of them don't because they are not good at expressing themselves. How right they are!

What is the point of getting involved in an institution which tries to cramp their style! But, how wrong they are! They are dismissing the Church for the wrong reasons. I would like to give them the right reasons. I would like to try to put those reasons into just three points: three dogmas which are the *catholic* dogmas par excellence, the three things that every apologetic effort should place clearly before the minds of both the waverer and the enquirer, three doctrines which do inter-relate and without which there really is no Church, three really shocking things, which epitomise not only the doctrine but also the practice of Christian religion.

And the first of these is the Eucharist.

THE SCANDAL OF THE EUCHARIST

You do realise, Ino, surely, what the Eucharist is supposed to be, you do remember, or could it be that this is something your religious education did not go into? The Eucharist is the changing of bread and wine, by an ordained priest, into the body and blood, soul and divinity of Christ. What was bread and wine before the consecration of the Mass, now only looks like bread and wine; in fact it is Christ's body and blood; he is now really, truly and substantially present — the live Jesus Christ, son of Mary, who once lived and died and then rose again and is alive forever in heaven and on the altar of the Church where he makes himself nourishment for the Christian. All this occurs at the Mass (which explains why people go to Mass, more or less often); and the presence of Christ remains when the Eucharist is reserved in the tabernacle (which explains why people go in and out of Catholic churches: John Paul II looks for the churches to be filled also *outside the times of Masses*).

Ino: independently of whether all this is true or not, this is what the Catholic Church believes to be true and what it teaches to be true. Is it not amazing and shocking that anyone nowadays could believe in 'transubstantiation' (that is the best technical theological term the Church has come up with to describe the changing of the bread-wine into Jesus Christ)? Maybe Catholics don't talk about it very much, or are not good at 'explaining' it or spelling it out — but that, anyway, is the vertiginous centre of the Catholic religion, the mysterious core, its secret event.

The Eucharist is one of seven sacraments, the normal channels by which God's supernatural grace reaches people, the visible signs of invisible grace, but whereas the other sacraments confer grace, this sacrament *contains* the author of grace. Here is another dimension: bread and wine are transformed into a living man, a man-God. For every good pagan man is man, and God is God — way over everything, Lord and Creator of all. But for the catholic Church God is Christ: the ever-existing trancendental God, maker of all things, became, and remains, a man. Now, it is difficult enough, it would seem, these days to get people to recognise the natural God, Creator and Lord. But the catholic Church teaches dogmatically that Jesus of Nazareth *is* the metaphysical son of God and is made present in the Eucharist (where he is liable to be mistreated by neglect and even abuse in churches of all kinds from adobe to marble, with spires piercing the clouds, like Cologne's, to churches underground in the modern catacombs).

And there is more still: the Eucharist is made in the 'sacrifice' of the Mass: the catholic Church teaches that the man-God, who walked the earth at a particular time in history, saved all men by his free suffering and death on the Cross and then rose from the dead. Before dying he anticipated his death at the Last Supper where he first turned food and drink into his body and blood; after his resurrection the *same* sacrifice of the Cross is re-presented in an unbloody way every time the Mass is celebrated. Thus the making of the Eucharist is a form of the arch-atonement, the great event of history whose effects can be appropriated by every person desirous of saving grace. Not only does transubstantiation happen (which is dramatic enough); not only is the Mass the Atonement Now (which relates that happening to a whole world in need of redemption — because it is a *dis-grace,* as is evident to everyone who looks around him); but through taking the Euch-arist, the individual person develops intimate communion with the God-man.

All this is the Eucharist, the Sacrament par excellence, according to Catholic teaching. And in one way or another all the other sacraments stem from or lead to the Eucharist. Baptism applies the grace of the atonement to the pagan soul, opening the door and setting him on the way to heaven and giving him access to the Eucharist.

The sacrament of penance in its primary purpose applies the grace of atonement to the baptised sinner who has cut himself off from God's friendship — giving him once more access to Com-munion, to the mysteries of the Eucharist. This sacrament of con-trite confession of sins to a priest means that the person must go physically to the Church, to Christ present in the priest, to ac-knowledge how he has sinned against faith or the laws of morality (i.e. he cannot in the normal course obtain forgiveness unless he goes through the judicial process). One logical consequence of this reconciliation is access to the Eucharist, Communion.

The sacrament of order is designed to provide the Church with people designated by Christ to (i) make the Eucharist and (ii) reconcile sinners via the sacrament of penance. That is why we have bishops and priests: they are according to Catholic teaching *necessary* for the Church to keep going; they constitute a special class of fallible people who form the hierarchy of the Church — distinct from the lay people. Bishops and priests are not a sort of extra the Catholics have which the Calvinists, for example, don't have: they are absolutely essential to the catholic Church: they are the way the Eucharist happens and the way to give access to the Eucharist.

Confirmation is a sacrament strengthening the Christian for adult life — life nourished by the Eucharist — and apostolate — attracting people to the Eucharist. Anointing of the sick is often combined with the final Eucharist of a person's life. And marriage is a Christian hallowing of husband and wife with a view to the creation of the domestic church — the human cell of the Church which brings children to faith and Communion.

From this we can see that sacramentally the Church is wholly about the Eucharist: all the paraphernalia, all the liturgy (which may not turn you on), all the embarassing unctiousness of a liturgy performed to make it a meaningful community event, all the institution of the Church with whatever encrustations it carries in any particular epoch, all its impediments of history, all its ups and downs over the centuries: the whole shooting gallery is nothing more and nothing less than the entourage and cultural setting of the Eucharist. Take away the Eucharist and none of this other stuff makes any sense. Leave this other stuff and the only sense it has is that it provides for the making of the Eucharist and for giving people access to that Sacrament.

Of course there are other Christian things; of course, every thing in the world can be Christianised. But a church — in Catholic theology — warrants the name of church only if it has the Eucharist: churches out of communion with the catholic Church are identified as such by having the Eucharist. If the Eucharist is missing what is left is a very very imperfect shadow of the people of God. Whereas if the Eucharist is there, then *the* Christian thing is going on, even if there are scandalous abuses. The pale shadow still has substance — the treasure of noble Christian behaviour, of good works, of fine ideals, of baptismal grace, of the word of God in the Bible — but the core is missing, the centre is empty, the centre is soft. Whereas the Catholic centre is the mystery of the real presence of the God-man, the crux of Christian belief.

Therefore, do not think that you are sweeping away the catholic Church when you dismiss the institution. In a sense you have done just that — you have swept away the One Thing Necessary (if you do away with hierarchy, for example): but you are making the Great Mistake: you have not understood what the Institution is about; you have failed to see through the pomp to the secret mystery. You have let yourself be shocked by the wrong things.

What you should be scandalised about is the right thing — the only thing really worth being scandalised about: the Catholic doctrine of the Eucharist. Not that I want you to be scandalised; but I have put you in the best position to be scandalised — because I have offered no apologia for the Eucharist (as you can imagine, if the Church is all about the Eucharist, then the Church over its long history must have made a marvellous apologia, but that is another story). I have merely indicated what the Church teaches the Eucharist to be. But if you *were* scandalised by the Eucharist, then at least you would be in the same class as many who heard this teaching from Jesus' own mouth — as you can read in chapter six of John's Gospel. They objected: 'This is a hard saying; who can listen to it?' (He called, in witnesses to the truth of this teaching, the future event of his ascension into heaven after his resurrection) 'After this many of his disciples drew back and no longer went about with him'. Who stayed behind? 'Jesus said to the twelve, Will you also go away?' and on behalf of the twelve, the future hierarchical, completely human, core of the Church, 'Simon Peter answered him, Lord to whom shall we go? You have the words of eternal life'.

The doctrine of the Eucharist, at its very first enunciation, sorted out those who were around Jesus. If you, Ino, are to be sorted out, then let it be on the score of the Eucharist and not on the attitude of some ecclesiastic — or many ecclesiastics — to some political situation or because some practising Catholics put you off by the way they behave — in your home, at art school, in a truthful history book or in the theoretical dreams your fertile mind weaves.

In sum: for any Catholic, now as before, the thing necessary is to be in the state of grace, to be able to attend and receive the Eucharist, the objective, reliable pledge of eternal life. Even if he is spiritually anaemic, that is what he really hungers for, 'the living bread which came down from heaven . . . he who eats this bread will live for ever, and the bread which I shall give for the life of the world is my flesh. Unless you eat the flesh of the Son of man and drink his blood, you have no life in you; he who eats my flesh and drinks my blood has eternal life, and I will raise him up on the last day.' Not a metaphor, not a parable, not a bread which has acquired a new 'meaning', not a bread which subjectively becomes for us the body of Christ, not a symbol: as the American catholic novelist, Flannery O'Connor, put it so precisely: 'if it's a symbol, to hell with it'.[1] The Eucharist is a hard saying: but it is, as far as sacraments go, *the only thing the Church is about.*

I spoke about there being three dogmas which essentially identify the catholic Church: three teachings which, if you want to dismiss the Church, you should primarily take issue with.

Not only one: for the Eucharist is to be found outside the visible confines of the catholic Church: certainly in the Orthodox Church — so much so that the catholic Church will direct you to the Greek Eucharist should you fail to find the Eucharist made by a Catholic priest.

The second dogma I will call *the infallibility of the pope.*

THE SCANDAL OF THE INFALLIBILITY OF THE POPE

The catholic Church projects itself as being the Church Christ founded, the true Church, the Church. The most recent dogmatic formulation of this teaching is to be found in the Vatican II document *Lumen gentium*. This teaching not only claims that there is historical continuity between an early Church founded by Christ and the catholic Church as it is today: it means it is the same Church essentially: any differences are superficial. To be a Catholic now means essentially the same as to be a Catholic in A.D. 40. If it did not the catholic Church would be a nonsense.

This teaching, for one thing, stresses that the Eucharist now is the same event as the first Eucharist and as the death and resurrection of Christ: the 'mysteries', the holy rites, are the very same. That in itself is a great claim: but on what authority is the claim made? You see, mysterious rites, taken in themselves, are just that; they have their parallel in many religions and pseudo-religions, although the Christian rites are very sophisticated and in no way pander to people's interest in the bizarre, the occult or the passionate.

But alongside and integrated with the Christian ministry of the Eucharist (governed and performed, we have seen, by the hierarchy of bishops and priests) there is another ministry — that of the word. This is the intellectual, doctrinal and moral dimension of the Church. Not only does the Church perform rites: it explains the rites that it performs, and because its rites are so holy (the scandal of the Eucharist) it warns Christians not to approach the

Eucharist, not to take the Eucharist unworthily i.e. in a state of sin (sin against right faith or sin against right morality: in other words, without having their consciences judged and their souls shriven).

The ministry of the word — which is also a part of the mission of the hierarchy — consists in the authoritative preaching of the Gospel, of the 'truth which sets you free.' Christ is not only 'the life' of mankind (through the Eucharist), he is 'the way', through his example and moral teaching, and 'the truth', in that in his person he contains all the elements of the faith, all the doctrine revealed by God. The catholic Church is about the truth about God (to which we must logically associate the right way of moral behaviour required for following Christ). The Church, in other words, contains, offers, all the truths to which we must necessarily subscribe if we are to obtain salvation. By 'we' I mean certainly Catholics: it is possible for people who are not Catholics or Christians to be saved (again, this is the teaching of the Church): but it is not possible for Catholics to be in God's grace if we knowlingly refuse to confess the truths of faith which the Church teaches us.

This hold of the Church on truth means that the Church is infallible, that is to say, it is preserved by God from error in proposing truths necessary for salvation. This is all very logical. As Cardinal Newman put it: Why is the catholic Church the only Church possibly worth belonging to? The only Church possibly worth belonging to is the Church which claims to be infallible. The only Church which claims to be infallible is the catholic Church. Therefore the catholic Church is the only Church possibly worth belonging to.

When the Church says it is infallible it says that what it teaches is true in an *objective* sense, i.e. true independently of any individual's *subjective* interpretation of what is true. This is very interesting — especially in modern times when fashionable philosophy would have us believe that there is no such thing as (objective) truth: it says what is true is whatever is true for you, whatever is meaningful to you, whatever makes sense for you. That kind of philosophy, which affects all of us to some degree, proposes that each person 'makes' his truth and therefore really there is no communication between two individuals. It's not such a new idea really: you will remember that when Jesus claimed to be the truth, Pilate his judge jeeringly asked: 'What is truth?' There are of course philosophers — including non-Christians — who do not profess this kind of subjectivist philosophy; but they are not in the majority. They would feel very lonely indeed in the modern world if there were not the catholic Church — and teeming millions of Catholics

– who are quite clear in their minds that there is such a thing as objective truth and that an individual can lay hold of it.

I should mention that there are other philosophers – marxists for example – who, for all the political claims they make about 'knowing' the way to go, are sheer materialists: they cannot *know*, because where all is matter, there is no place for thought, no room for any spiritual action, any human ability to transcend matter and grasp the essence and meaning of the world around them.

Anyway, the Church tells us that it is infallible. And in so doing it is claiming complete and adequate continuity with the Church established by Christ on Peter – 'Thou art Peter and upon this rock I will build my Church' – and on the commission by Christ to his apostles: 'All authority in heaven and on earth has been given to me. Go, therefore, make disciples of all the nations; baptise them in the name of the Father and of the Son and of the Holy Spirit, and teach them to observe all the commands I gave you. And know that I am with you always; yes, to the end of time' (Mt 28:19-20). Note here again that this is the same Christ, in the same gospels, who was depicted in the nineteenth century as the dreamy gentle 'knocker on the door' and in the twentieth as the radical who condemned the Pharisees and threw the money changers out of the Temple. Don't make the mistake of creating, selectively, from the gospels a Christ of your own: try to take in the whole Christ – the sayings which seem hard to you and the sayings which seem soft. The Bible has come to us through the Church (and the Jews) and its authentic interpretation also comes through the Church: otherwise we are back in subjectivism, the heretical subjectivisim of Protestantism's *sola Scriptura,* scripture alone.

But even if we accept that the Church is infallible, how to recognise where its infallible teaching is? There are difficulties – if one is left to explore two thousand years of church history to sift the essential from the inessential; there are theological problems in assessing the meanings of the Creeds, for example, which the Church has used over the centuries. But the normal Catholic is not expected to be a theological researcher, for the Church itself has pointed to two particular instances of infallibility – certain instances of the common teaching of the bishops in Council (always with at least the implicit agreement of the bishop of Rome), *and* the teaching of the Bishop of Rome on his own, in certain circumstances. This latter instance is *the infallibility of the Pope*.

The infallibility of the pope is a dogma which was defined in 1870, at Vatican I. This does not mean that it is a teaching, binding on Catholics, which was created in 1870: the only teaching that any Catholic worth his salt would subscribe to with full free assent is one which has been part and parcel of the doctrine of the faith from the very beginning (if the Church could 'make' truths rather than just explicate them, 'truth' would be its creature; whereas the Church is the truth only in the sense that the truth is entrusted to it by Christ as something objective and unchanging). History witnesses to this charism of the pope, just as it witnesses to the truth of the Eucharist.

The teaching of the Church on the infallibility of the pope is that the bishop of Rome is preserved from error when he teaches *ex cathedra* (in his most formal way) doctrine on faith or morals to be held by the whole Church.

I want you to note the radical arrogance of the Church in defining this doctrine: it has made it clear, on pain of the penalties of heresy, on pain of being barred from the Eucharist, that Catholics are required by God to believe certain statements enuntiated by the pope: not by the whole Church, not via surveys or investigations, but by *a* man. This is what Catholics believe; this is the scandal you might well take issue with if you really want to object to the catholic Church.

Who is this man, this pope? The horror of the doctrine is that it could be anyone, anyone who has become bishop of Rome, no matter how human his manoeuvrings, no matter how sub-standard his personal life: and there are instances of popes who were less than edifying, shall we say? Don't ask me to give instances. It is all documented: it is all history and that means that in the future as well as in the past we may have popes who are bad people. Is it surprising? Not at all. The pope, any pope, is a mere man: he is you, capable of all the most horrifying of sins. I don't know what is horrifying to you — you may be a very good person who has always been very good — but have you not noticed the attraction of evil? Yet is there anything more horrifying than to see an intimate of Jesus, one of his closest friends, someone who swore he would never deny him, flip over, simply because his skin was at risk, and say he *never knew him*: this was the sin of Peter, already an apostle, hours before confirmed in his role (at least implicitly) as the leader of the apostles. Subsequent history has nothing to teach the Church: it is all there, in the gospel accounts.

All this means that the Church survives, remains faithful, irrespective of the infidelity of its officers; irrespective, we might say, of its humanity (which is all warts, when compared with its divinity). Somehow, despite the fallible human element in the Church, God acts, making it always the pure channel of its grace — the grace of the Eucharistic mystery and the grace of the Word of God.

This is what Catholics believe: that the focus of authority, the assessor of truth, is a mere fallible man. Does this doctrine not smack of the same arrogance of truth as the doctrine of the Eucharist? Not only does the Church say that truth is attainable, not only does it say that it has, that it is, the truth: it really pins its colours to the mast and leaves us no escape — leaves itself no escape — by pointing to a physical location of truth in the world, saying that its high priest is God's mouthpiece, the epiphany of Christ, 'sweet Christ on earth,' as Catherine of Siena called him. (Catherine of Siena, a mere Catholic, was no kow-tower to the pope: she bullied him and badgered him to leave the lotus farm of Avignon and face into the political anarchy of the Rome of his time: she experienced the cowardice of the pope of her time but this did not cloud her faith that he took Christ's place on earth).

This — only this, all this — is what the catholic Church is about. When I refer you to the 'infallibility' of the pope I am directing you really to his authority, to the doctrine that without him the Church is (would be) desolate — fatherless, condemned to disunity and strife. The pope's infallibility is only the summit of his authority; in everyday life he (in continuity with his predecessors) is the contemporary most authentic assessor of the Church's tradition, the arch re-presenter for the present generation of the perennial truths of faith. He — and the bishops in communion with him — presents to us the doctrine of Christ: Christ's doctrine about man (and that implies morality) and his doctrine about God (the doctrine of the Trinity which leads to the doctrine of the Eucharist).

To put it another way: for 'the Church' to make any sense, it must be unique: there must be only one Church. 'The Church' can never be an atomised collection of groupings of Christians, each independent of the others, each self-defining. Undoubtedly these groupings — which do exist — have *some* relationships with each other, extrinsic or even intrinsic. But the great, confused array of Christian churches and communities and sects: *that* is not 'the Church'. Only *one* of all those entities is *'the Church'*. As a pope of the last century pointed out, 'because all Christians needed to be united by a common, unchanging faith, our Lord Jesus Christ, through his prayers, obtained for Peter the grace that in the exercise of his authority his faith should never fail' (Leo XIII, *Satis cognitum*): the Church, to be, to subsist, to keep going, to be itself, to keep its identity always, needs to be preserved from error.

The doctrine of infallibility and of the teaching authority of the Church — the magisterium — is not quite as simple as all this. But the Church does teach that the pope is infallible in certain circumstances and the bishop of Rome is the necessary cornerstone of the unity and of apostolic authority in the Church; and obviously that infallibility and authority are linked. It is in view of the pope's authority that the Holy Spirit protects him against error. The main point I am making here is that *someone* — the Church —is claiming to *know* the truth: and no one else in the world makes the same claim.

Do not worry, at this point, at the possible implications (for your life) of this infallible authority: focus for a while on the very core of what the Church is: Eucharist-Truth.

THE PRESUMPTION OF ASSUMPTION

If you were to press me to add just one more element to the core of the Catholic religion, a third thing and last thing to add to the true checklist of what the Church is, what it is about, what the Catholic religion really is — the essence of Catholicism and nothing to do with the essence of the sects, I will give it to you readily. I will call it the dogma of the assumption of Mary using that as a portfolio dogma concerning the place of Mary in the Church.

The dogma of the assumption states that at the end of her earthly life Mary the mother of Jesus was taken up body and soul into heaven; and there she lives as queen of the universe, mother of the Church, endowed with numberless prerogatives and titles.

I have chosen this particular Marian dogma for several reasons.

The second reason is that it is incontrovertibly *the* example of the exercise of papal infallibility, the only clear instance since 1870 when a pope has used (in 1950 to be exact) his full authority to proclaim a dogma of faith; a Catholic, because he goes along with papal infallibility, goes along with the doctrine of the assumption; if a Catholic rejected this doctrine he would be rejecting the Church and entering a sect (and in the process he would leave the body of Mary rotted away into the dust of Asia Minor).

The third reason is that this dogma is not to be found in any explicit way in Scripture; it is itself an assertion of tradition ('hand ing on') of the faith, whereby revealed truth is passed on either physically (by way of rites, for example) or orally (but not initially in written form). It is also a doctrine which some theologians were uncertain about prior to its definition — just as Aquinas, the great Doctor, was uncertain about Mary's immaculate conception (*defined* centuries after his death). Thus it is a very good indicator of the role of and need for Church authority as something which sifts and assesses scripture and tradition and gives an authentic interpretation; it is a clear reminder that the *Church* is the thing as far as Catholics are concerned.

The fourth reason is that it installs in heaven a *mere* human, the first of a multitude of *mere* men and women whom Catholics alive today confidently expect to join. Jesus Christ, man and God, did rise from the dead and ascend into heaven; but with the assumption of Mary *mere* man is no longer confined to the limits of earthly existence or the disembodied (and unnatural) existence of spirits — which is the state of all the *souls* in heaven. The doctrine of the assumption of Mary body and soul gives the rest of us, as we are, a place in heaven in the person of Mary.

And the first reason for choosing this as the third dogma is that it has to do with Mary, the woman who is unstained by any trace of sin from the moment of her conception, the woman who did not sin, the girl who was prepared to be the mother of the Messiah, who in turn proved to be the metaphysical son of God (perfect God) who took on human nature (becoming perfectly a man) — the mother of God. On the feastday of her birth the Church praises her birthday as 'marking the dawn of our salvation'. The Church celebrates Mary? Yes. But Mary's is a reflected glory.

There is a folk-praise of heroes whereby the woman in the crowd shouts out 'Blessed is the womb that bore you' or 'Blessed is the mother who gave birth to you'. (The very words were used to Christ.) And the interesting thing is that this praise of the mother is in fact the height of praise of the son: how better could someone praise *you* than by shouting 'Blessed is the mother who bore you'? She is blessed and praised as the best way of praising you: her glory is *your* existence and *your* beauty and the achievements of *your* life.

Indeed, in the case of human heroes, direct praise is declined by the best of them (for despite their achievements they know too well, in their heart, that any such praise must ultimately be referred to God) but if it is the mother who is praised, well ... : there is a slight disclaimer there of laurels being one's very own. When this bit of folk-praise was addressed to Christ he was very quick to point out, 'Blessed are they rather who hear the word of God and keep it': This can be interpreted as meaning that Mary's right to praise was more for her humility and obedience to God's word than to the physical fact of being his mother; but it also in her case can refer to her being the hearer *par excellence* of the word of God which asked her to receive in her womb the Word of God, his very son, and to shape his human existence. Whichever interpretation applies, it all leads to the fact that the Church we are talking about *is not* without Mary: she and the Church go together, they are intimately and inextricably linked. The truth about Mary is at the core of the Catholic religion.

Three dogmas, three tests of the catholic Church; it is the Church of the three: Peter, Mary, Jesus; the catholic Christians are those who go *omnes ad Jesum cum Petro per Mariam:* all towards Jesus, with Peter, through Mary. Do not, then, say that I have burdened you with three theological dogmas, with some sort of formal checklist or litmus paper for testing the Church. I have pointed out to you, simply, three people: Jesus, Mary, Peter: as summing up all the truth, all the mystery, all the security, all the warmth, the whole focus of affection of the people of God. These three names, on your lips or in your mind can be the prayer of both the committed and the estranged Catholic. And prayer not argument is what draws to dwell in man's very soul.

IF YOU STEP ASIDE FROM THE CHURCH LET IT BE
FOR THE BEST REASONS; IF YOU ARE A CATHOLIC
BE ONE FOR THE RIGHT REASONS

Therefore, Ino, if you are going to take issue with the Church, take issue with the real Church, with what the Church is really about. know what you are knocking, know what you are taking leave of. Don't beat the air, don't fight phantoms, don't mistake the word for the trees. Be serious: examine the Church for what it is and for what it says it is: not for what you superficially think it is. There is the Church, really. A grouping of people laden with failings, people far more aware of their failings than those who in fact are wallowing in the darkness and anguish of not really knowing anything. The Church, a people who are pilgrims, striving, failing, stumbling: a people who are sinners who know they are sinners but who keep following the Holy Grail, believing it to be, knowing it by faith to be, a Grail which contains the Blood of Christ and the Bread of his truth.

You are a Catholic; somewhere in your soul you have the faith you received at baptism. No matter how astray your intellectual development has led you, no matter how your moral deviance has given you a distaste for the good life (that, I trust, has not happened), you are capable of making your own the teaching of the Church. I suspect that you will not easily reject the scandal of the Eucharist, the scandal of infallible teaching about faith *and morals* or the role of Mary. At least I warn you, if you do recognise that these identify the catholic Church at the core of Christianity, to treat them with the awe that is their due. For if you do knowingly reject them you will be left in a world which has no access to supernatural truth and no access to the centre of history, the incarnation of the Son of God. At best you will attain — also by God's good 'natural' graces — a knowledge that 'out there' a personal God exists who rewards good and punishes evil, and a very rough and ready idea of how to go about living the good life; but unfortunately life is short and you may never quite 'arrive', while your faithful brothers even now drink living waters which spring up to eternal life.

So much for apologetics: not that these lines have been an apologia: they have only been a kind of provocation to explore the treasury of the Church. But so much for apologetics. Apologetics is only one route to the revitalisation of faith; there are thousands of routes; and all of them really start not in the mind but in the soul who prays 'to God if there is a God', or to God 'I believe, but very very weakly: Lord, help my unbelief'.

The Blessed Eucharist

Charles Connolly

*'What is the mark of a Christian? That . . . he
be holy and blameless and so eat the Body of
Christ and drink his Blood'* (Saint Basil).

What a thing is determines what its meaning and purpose are and
what should be our attitude towards it. What, then, is the Eucharist? The Eucharist is one of the seven sacraments instituted by
Jesus Christ in which, under the appearances of bread and wine,
the second Person of the Most Blessed Trinity made man is present
with his body and blood, soul and divinity so that he might offer
himself in an unbloody manner to his heavenly Father in the sacrifice of the Mass (sacrificial dimension) and give himself to the
faithful as food for their souls (sacramental dimension).[1]

If this is what the Eucharist really is in itself, then this is what it
ought to be for us, namely a sacrifice and a sacrament. For the
Eucharist is not just one more item in the life of the Church and
the Christian, one thing among a host of others. No. It is *the* thing
which really counts, the centre and root of the life of the Church
and its members.

As Vatican Council II put it: 'But the other sacraments, and
indeed all ecclesiastical ministries and works of the apostolate are
bound up with the Eucharist and are directed towards it. For in
the most blessed Eucharist is contained the whole spiritual good of
the Church, namely Christ himself, our Pasch and the living bread
which gives life to men through his flesh — that flesh which is
given life and gives life through the Holy Spirit. Thus men are
invited and led to offer themselves, their works and all creation
with Christ. For this reason the Eucharist appears as the source
and the summit of all preaching of the Gospel: catechumens are
gradually led up to participation in the Eucharist, while the faithful who have already been consecrated in baptism and confirmation are fully incorporated in the Body of Christ by the reception of the Eucharist.'[2]

The dignity of this sacrament over the other six resides in the fact that, unlike the others, it is not only an instrument through which God bestows grace but it also contains substantially, Christ himself, who as God is the very author of grace.

Besides Eucharist (thanksgiving) other names are given to this sacrament:

— *Communion,* because as Saint Paul says 'the blessing cup that we bless is a communion with the blood of Christ, and the bread that we break is a communion with the body of Christ' (1 Cor 10:16).

— *Sacrament of love and peace,* because it enables us to love our enemies and put an end to hatred, dissension and discord.

— *Viaticum,* because it is a spiritual food by which we are sustained for our pilgrimage through life and strengthened especially at the moment of death.

— *Lord's Supper,* because this saving mystery of faith was instituted at the Last Supper.

Further names are the Table of the Lord, the Holy Sacrifice, the Holy of Holies, the Blessed Sacrament. Each of the names emphasises one or other aspect of the Eucharistic mystery: the Real Presence, the sacrifice of the Mass, the sacrament of Holy Communion. It is to these aspects that Pope John Paul II referred in his first encyclical when he said that the Eucharist is 'at one and the same time a Sacrifice-Sacrament, a Communion-Sacrament and a Presence-Sacrament' *(Redemptor hominis,* 20).

INSTITUTION

The institution of this sacrament is attested to by the evangelists Matthew, Mark and Luke, and by Saint Paul in his first epistle to the Corinthians: 'For this is what I received from the Lord, and in turn passed on to you: that on the same night that he was betrayed, the Lord Jesus took bread and thanked God for it and broke it and said: "This is my body, which is for you; do this as a memorial of me". In the same way he took the cup after supper and said: "This cup is the new covenant in my blood. Whenever you drink it do this as a memorial of me" ' (1 Cor 11:23-25).

The tradition which the Apostle of the Gentiles has entrusted to his recent converts in Corinth is precisely the same tradition that took root and was followed in the earliest days of the Church after Pentecost. The first Christian community is described as 'faithful to the teaching of the apostles, to the brotherhood, *to the breaking of bread* and to the prayers' (Acts 2:42).

The attitude of Christ — and this ought to be our attitude as well, for we are to follow in his footsteps (cf Phil 2:5) — to the paschal meal, which was to anticipate his sacrificial death on the Cross the following afternoon, is summed up in these words of Saint Luke: 'I have longed and longed to eat this passover with you before I suffer, because I tell you, I shall not eat it again until it is fulfilled in the kingdom of God' (Lk 22:15-16).

As has so often been said before no one should be surprised that Saint John, who gives a detailed account of the Last Supper, fails to mention the institution of the sacrament. There was no need for him to do so because, when writing at the end of the first century, his intention was to supplement what had already been said by the other three evangelists. Nor indeed was there any pressing reason to give details when Christians everywhere were celebrating the Eucharist as an integral part of their faith and practice. Saint Justin Martyr, an early apologist, describes their practice as follows: 'Then, bread and a chalice containing wine mixed with water are presented to the one presiding over the brethren. He takes them and offers praise and glory to the Father of all, through the name of the Son and of the Holy Spirit, and he recites lengthy prayers of thanksgiving to God in the name of those to whom he granted such favours. At the end of these prayers and thanksgiving, all present express their approval by saying "Amen." This Hebrew word, "Amen," means "So be it." And when he who presides has celebrated the Eucharist, they whom we call deacons permit each one present to partake of the Eucharist bread, and wine and water; and they carry it also to the absentees.' [3]

It is Saint John, the disciple whom Jesus loved, the one who laid his head on the Master's breast, who captures the intimate feelings of Christ's heart at the time of the institution of the Eucharist: 'It was before the festival of the Passover, and Jesus knew that the hour had come for him to pass from this world to the Father. He had always loved those who were his own in the world, but now he showed how perfect his love was' (Jn 13:1).

'This is the source of the joy we feel on Holy Thursday — the realization that the creator has loved his creatures to such an extent. Our Lord Jesus Christ, as though all the other proofs of his mercy were insufficient, institutes the Eucharist so that he can always be close to us. We can only understand up to a point that he does so because Love moves him, who needs nothing, not to want to be separated from us. The Blessed Trinity has fallen in love with man, raised to the level of grace and made "to God's image and likeness." ' [4]

In the definition of the Eucharist given above it was stated that Jesus Christ was present with his body and blood. This eucharistic presence is not the only presence he has in his Church but it is 'the supreme form'. [5]

Pope Paul VI has reminded us that Christ is present in the Church when she is

(a)   at prayer;
(b)   engaged in works of mercy;
(c)   proclaiming the word of God;
(d)   occupied in ruling and governing God's people;
(e)   offering the sacrifice of the Mass and administering the sacraments. [6]

While all these various presences are real and not fictitious or imaginary, yet only his presence in the Eucharist is rightly termed 'real' for 'by reason of its excellence it is the substantial presence by which Christ is made present without doubt, whole and entire, God and Man.' [7]

The dogma of the real presence, 'the confession of the truth of this real presence, and of the real substantial change of bread and wine into Christ's body and blood, is the most insistent test and exercise of our faith; it is a constant, intransigent call to the all-important humility of faith, confronting all, priests and laity, in their daily lives. From the beginning, our Lord made acceptance of this hard saying the decisive test of those who would follow him (Jn 6:60-69). If the intervention of divine power in our material world by the Eucharistic transmutation of substance scandalizes the preconceptions of human reason, so does that other astounding irruption of the divine into this physical world, which we call the Incarnation. The two mysteries of faith are closely linked. The real presence of Christ in the flesh under the sacramental veil draws its meaning from that primary sacrament of the Incarnation, God really present in human flesh.' [8]

The earliest opponents of this truth of our faith were the Docetists who, not believing in the real incarnation of the Word of God, were logically forced not to believe in the real presence of his body and blood in the Eucharist. As a consequence they abandoned the sacrament: 'They abstain from the Eucharist and the prayer (i.e. the Eucharistic prayer) because they do not believe that the Eucharist is the flesh of our Saviour Jesus Christ which suffered for our sins and which the Father in his bounty has raised up again'. [9]

At a much later date Berengarius of Tours (d. 1088) denied the real presence of Christ and the transubstantiation of the bread and wine. He held that Christ was merely symbolically present in the Eucharist, and his ideas, which he had inherited from Ratramnus (d. 868), have had their influence on nearly all the subsequent errors which have contradicted the traditional teaching of the Church, disturbed the minds of the faithful and caused them considerable mental confusion and distress in matters of faith. [10]

Retracting his error, Berengarius made the following profession of faith: 'I believe in my heart and openly profess that the bread and wine placed upon the altar are, by the mystery of the sacred prayer and the words of the Redeemer, substantially changed into the true and life-giving flesh and blood of Jesus Christ our Lord, and that after the consecration, there is present the true body of Christ which was born of the Virgin and, offered up for the salvation of the world, hung on the cross and now sits at the right hand of the Father, and that there is present the true blood of Christ which flowed from his side. They are present not only by means of a sign and of the efficacy of the sacrament, but also in the very reality and truth of their nature and substance.' [11]

REAL, TRUE, SUBSTANTIAL PRESENCE

By 'real presence' we mean simply that 'in the blessed sacrament of the Holy Eucharist, after the consecration of the bread and wine, our Lord Jesus Christ, true God and man, is truly, really and substiantially present under the perceptible species of bread and wine'. [12]

The words 'truly, really and substiantially' are used by the Council of Trent for a very precise reason: to counteract the teaching of three different Protestant errors:

(a) Zwingli: he denied the real presence and stated that the bread and wine were mere symbols of the body and blood of Christ. He describes what he means in the following terms: 'just as a man about to set out on a journey might give to his wife a most precious ring upon which his portrait is engraved, saying "Behold your husband; thus you may keep him and delight in him even though he is absent", so our Lord Jesus Christ, as he departed, left to his spouse the Church his own image in the sacrament of the supper'. [13]

In other words what Zwingli teaches is the *real absence* of Jesus Christ in the sacrament, not the real presence. The Catholic

Church uses the word *true* to oppose this error.

(b)   Other Protestants held that Christ was present in the Eucharist only through faith, i.e. the sacrament aroused the faith of the community because it helped us to recall what our Saviour did for us at the Last Supper on the night he was betrayed. So when Trent say *really* present, it means present independently of those present at the liturgical celebration and of their faith, and of those who receive the sacrament. *We* do not make him present; rather through the very power of consecration bestowed on his priests Christ makes himself present.

(c)   Calvin taught a dynamic presence of Christ in the Holy Eucharist, i.e. through the sacrament Christ influences the predestined faithful with a power which emanates from his glorified body in heaven. No, says the Church. It is not a mere presence of power, but a *substantial* presence.

Luther too had his own particular ideas regarding the Blessed Eucharist. He admitted what he called a real presence but Christ was present only for as long as the liturgical celebration was in progress. As soon as it was finished, the bread and wine were once more only simple bread and wine. During the celebration, he taught, the true body and blood of Christ co-existed with the bread and wine, but there was never — to his mind — any truth in the Church's assertion that the bread and wine were transubstantiated into the Body and Blood of Christ. 'In this sacrament [the Eucharist] the bread is truly transubstantiated into the body of the Lord Jesus Christ and the wine into his blood':[14] so teaches the Council of Lyons in 1274 A.D. 'When our Lord himself declares, as our faith teaches us, that his flesh is food indeed, what room can remain for doubt concerning the real presence of his body and blood?' asks Saint Augustine.

The immediate consequence of the real presence is that we see how perfect is the new covenant established by Christ as compared to the shadows of the law of Moses, and so with faith that is firm and unwavering we glimpse and adore God made Man present with us, not visible to the naked eye but under the veil of the sacred mysteries. 'My delight is to be with the sons of men' (Prov. 8:31).

TRADITION

There can be no doubt that 'the bread over which thanksgiving is pronounced is the body of the Lord, and the chalice of his blood.'[16] It is the constant teaching of the Fathers of the Church.

Witness Saint John Chrysostom: 'Let us then in everything believe God and gainsay him in nothing, though what is said may seem to be contrary to our thoughts and senses, but let his word be of higher authority than both reasonings and sight. Thus let us do in the Mysteries also, not looking at the things set before us, but keeping in mind his sayings. For his word cannot deceive, but our senses are easily beguiled. That has never failed, but these in most things go astray. Since the word says, "This is my body," let us both be persuaded and believe, and look at it with the eyes of our mind.' [17]

'How many now say, I would wish to see his form, his shape, his clothes, his shoes. Look: you see him, you touch him, you eat him. And you indeed desire to see his clothes, but he gives himself to you, not to see only, but also to touch and eat and receive within you . . .Look therefore, lest you also yourself become guilty of the body and blood of Christ. They [i.e. the Jews who crucified him] slaughtered the all-holy body, but you receive it in a filthy soul after such great benefits. For neither was it enough for him to be made man, to be smitten and slaughtered, but he also indeed makes us his body . . .There are often mothers that after the travail of birth send out their children to other women to be nursed; but he endures not to do this, but himself feeds us with his own blood, and by all means entwines us with himself.' [18]

'We become one body, and members of his flesh and of his bones. Let the initiated follow what I say. In order then that we may become this not by love only but in very deed, let us be blended into that flesh. This is brought about by the food which he has freely given us, desiring to show the love that he bears us. On this account he has mingled himself with us; he has kneaded his body with ours that we might become one thing, like a body joined to the head . . . He has given to those who desire him not only to see him, but even to touch and eat him, to fix their teeth in his flesh and to embrace him and satisfy all their love. Parents often entrust their offspring to others to feed; "But I," he says, do not so. I feed you with my own flesh, desiring that you all be nobly born . . . For he that gives himself to you here much more will do so hereafter. I have willed to become your brother, for your sake I shared in flesh and blood, and in turn I give to you that same flesh and blood by which I became your kinsman." ' [19]

Also very much to the point is the explanation of the Eucharist given by Saint Justin Martyr in his apology for the Christian faith: 'We call this food the Eucharist, of which only he can partake who has acknowledged the truth of our teachings, who has been cleansed by baptism for the remission of his sins and for his regeneration, and who regulates his life upon the principles laid down by Christ. Not as ordinary bread or as ordinary drink do we partake of them, but just as, through the word of God, our Saviour Jesus Christ became Incarnate and took upon himself flesh and blood for our salvation, so, we have been taught, the food which has been made the Eucharist by the prayer of his word, and which nourishes our flesh and blood by assimilation, is both the flesh and blood of that Jesus who was made flesh. The Apostles in their memoirs, which are called Gospels, have handed down what Jesus ordered them to do; that he took bread and, after giving thanks, said: "Do this in remembrance of me; for this is my body." In like manner, he took also the chalice, gave thanks, and said: "This is my blood", and to them only did he give it.' [20]

This does not mean that every single statement of the Fathers is a clear, straightforward assertion of the real presence. Individual passages have to be read in context and bearing in mind the overall teaching of the writer. For example, Saint Augustine and other Fathers sometimes speak of the Eucharist as the sign of Christ's body and blood; they refer to the symbol of the Eucharist and talk of a 'spiritual eating' of Christ. And indeed this is all true, for the external element of the Eucharist, i.e. the appearances of bread and wine, have as their proper function to signify the body and blood of Jesus which are really, is invisibly, present. The phrase 'spiritual eating' is used to differentiate between taking ordinary nourishment for the good of the body and the reception of Holy Eucharist, which nourishes the soul, and to stress the need for both faith and charity on the part of the recipient if the sacrament is to be fully effective.

Vatican Council II also sees the Eucharist as the sign and symbol of unity because 'really sharing in the body of the Lord in the breaking of the Eucharistic bread we are taken up into communion with him and one another'. [21] Saint Thomas gives us a more than adequate summary as to why Christ is in this sacrament in very truth and not merely in a figure or sign: 'The presence of Christ's true body and blood in this sacrament cannot be detected by sense, nor understanding, but by faith alone, which rests upon Divine authority. Hence, on Luke 22:19 "This is my body, which shall be delivered up for you," Cyril says: "Doubt not whether this be true; but take rather the Saviour's words with faith; for since he is the Truth, he does not lie."

'Now this is suitable, first for the perfection of the New Law. For, the sacrifices of the Old Law contained only in figure that true sacrifice of Christ's Passion, according to Heb 10:11 "For the law having a shadow of the good things to come, not the very image of the things." And therefore it was necessary that the sacrifice of the New Law instituted by Christ should have something more, namely, that it should contain Christ himself crucified, not merely in signification or figure, but also in very truth. And therefore this sacrament which contains Christ himself, as Dionysius says *(Eccl. Hier. iii),* is perfective of all the other sacraments, in which Christ's virtue is participated.

'Secondly, this belongs to Christ's love, out of which for our salvation he assumed a true body of our nature. And because it is the special feature of friendship to live together with friends, as the Philosopher says *(Ethic. ix),* He promises us his bodily presence as a reward, saying (Mt 24:28). "Where the body is, there shall the eagles be gathered together." Yet meanwhile in our pilgrimage he does not deprive us of his bodily presence; but unites us with himself in this sacrament through the truth of his body and blood. Hence (Jn 6:57) he says: "He that eats my flesh, and drinks my blood, abides in me, and I in him." Hence this sacrament is the sign of supreme charity, and the uplifter of our hope, from such familiar union of Christ with us.

'Thirdly, it belongs to the perfection of faith, which concerns his humanity just as it does his Godhead, according to Jn 14:1: "You believe in God, believe also in Me." And since faith is of things unseen, as Christ shows us his Godhead invisibly, so also in this sacrament he shows us his flesh in an invisible manner.

'Some men accordingly, not paying heed to these things, have contended that Christ's body and blood are not in this sacrament except as in a sign, a thing to be rejected as heretical, since it is contrary to Christ's words. Hence Berengarius, who had been the first deviser of this heresy, was afterwards forced to withdraw his error, and to acknowledge the truth of the faith.' [22]

HOLY SCRIPTURE

This teaching of the Fathers and Doctors of the Church is a theological reflexion on the teaching of Scripture.

On one occasion in Capharnaum our Lord went out of his way to instruct his followers on the nature, meaning and purpose of the sacrament which he was later to institute at the Last Supper.

St John tells us that he multiplied five barley loaves and fed five thousand people. 'I have pity on all these people; they have been with me for three days now and have nothing to eat. I do not want to send them off hungry, they might collapse on the way' (Mt 15:32). So great was the miracle, that they all ate and were satisfied, and twelve baskets were left with the left-overs. 'As a grain of wheat slowly multiplies in the ground, so the bread and fishes by a divinely hastened process were multiplied until everyone had his fill . . .Nature was to go as far as it could, then God supplied the rest . . . In the reckoning of men there is always a deficit; in the arithmetic of God there is always a surplus'. [23]

Incredible! Unless you were there and actually saw it happen, or like us, accept it as true on faith in the testimony of an eye-witness, Saint John. In the hands of the Lord bread is no longer subject to the ordinary physical laws of nature.

That evening to the astonishment of his apostles he walked on the waters of the lake. 'They saw Jesus walking on the lake and coming towards the boat' (Jn 6:19). Incredible! Yes, unless you were in the boat with the twelve or believed Saint John when he tells us that it actually happened. Once more the Lord's teaching is clear: 'I am in control of nature. My body is not subject to the laws of gravity, when I wish it not to be'.

Next day he brought his listeners to dwell explicitly, step by step, on the Eucharist. 'I tell you most solemnly, you are looking for me not because you have seen the signs but because you had all the bread you wanted to eat. Do not work for food that cannot last, but work for food that endures to eternal life, the kind of food the Son of Man is offering you' (Jn 6:26, 27).

And where is this bread to be found? 'I am the living bread which has come down from heaven. Anyone who eats this bread will live for ever; and the bread that I shall give is my flesh, for the life of the world . . . For my flesh is real food and my blood is real drink. He who eats my flesh and drinks my blood lives in me and I live in him' (Jn 6:51, 55-56).

A lack of faith was responsible for the desertion of many; they were unable to say with Simon Peter who, when he was asked 'What about you, do you wnat to go away too? , replied 'Lord, whom shall we go to? You have the message of eternal life, and we believe, we know you are the Holy One of God' (Jn 6:67-68).

It is the same lack of faith which nowadays would reduce the words of Christ to a metaphor, against all sound logic. That Christ must be taken literally is seen from

(a) his choice of words: real food, real drink, eat;
(b) the impossibility of giving a symbolic meaning to his words;
(c) the reaction of those who left. They understood exactly

what he meant. That is why they left. Had there been a simple misunderstanding or misinterpretation, undoubtedly Jesus would have clarified the matter. But no! He even took the risk of losing his Apostles rather than change his teaching.

The words Jesus used to institute the sacrament are a clear indication of what he was actually doing and have always been read in the Catholic Church with their literal meaning. 'Then he took some bread, and when he had given thanks, broke it and give it to them, saying: "This is my body which will be given for you; do this as a memorial of me." He did the same with the cup after supper, and said, "This cup is the new covenant in my blood which will be poured out for you" ' (Lk 22:19-20).

'And indeed it is difficult to see how the literal meaning of the words of Christ can be evaded. The solemnity of the occasion, the words used, the absence of any warning that a metaphor was intended, the very feebleness of the metaphor — if metaphor it was — all conspire to exclude the figurative sense of the words "this is my body." It is true that Christ had often used figures of speech, but they had either been so obviously such as to need no explanation or else Christ had carefully explained them lest the Apostles, simple-minded men, should be misled. Nor was the occasion one which called for ambiguity; on the contrary, it was precisely the moment for plain speaking. It had been necessary for him in the early days of his ministry to shroud his meaning under the form of parables, both to adapt himself to the minds of his hearers and in order to give an opportunity to men of good will to come and ask him to explain. But he was now at the last evening of his life on earth; he was surrounded, not by the suspicious Pharisees and Sadducees, but by his own faithful Apostles whom he trusted, to whom he spoke no more in parables, but plainly. If they failed to grasp his meaning now, they could not learn it from him on the morrow; for then he would be no more with them. He spoke plainly because he was instituting a new Testament, a new Law; and a testament, a covenant, is not formulated in figurative language. The Old Testament had been ratified by the blood of the victims, and Moses had sprinkled the people with it; the New Testament was ratified by the blood of Christ, of whom those victims had been but a type. Was the reality to be less perfect than the figure, the shadow more real than the substance? It was therefore the real blood of Christ which the Apostles reverently drank, the blood which was shed for the remission of sins; it was the true body of Christ which they ate, the body which was given for them, the flesh that was given for the life of the world.' [24]

TRANSUBSTANTIATION

Of late this word — transubstantiation — has fallen on hard times in spite of what Pope Paul VI had to say in the 'Creed of the People of God': 'In this Sacrament there is no other way in which Christ can be present except through the conversion of the entire substance of bread into his Body and through the conversion of the entire substance of wine into his Blood, leaving unchanged only those properties of bread and wine which are open to our senses. This hidden conversion is appropriately and justly called by the Church *transubstantiation*. Any theological explanation intent on arriving at some understanding of this mystery, if it is to be in accordance with Catholic faith, must maintain, without ambiguity, that in the order of reality which exists independently of the human mind, the bread and wine cease to exist after the consecration.'

Other less adequate words have been substituted on the basis that modern man no longer understands or thinks in terms of substance and accident, something which is wholly untrue once he is asked to reflect and is given a simple and clear idea of the meaning of these two terms.

'The Church has always held that after the consecration, only what looks like bread (the accidentals) remains; the actual bread (the substance) has been entirely replaced by the substance of the Lord's body.

'The difference between substance and accidentals may be illustrated as follows. If you grasp a bar of iron, you know what it is from its weight, colour and hardness. But if you take the bar out into space beyond the pull of gravity, it becomes weightless. If you place it in a furnace, it becomes a red-hot liquid. Is it still iron? Yes, for its substance remains the same, even though the accidentals have completely changed. The direct reversal takes place in the Eucharist: in the blast furnace of God's love at the consecration, the *accidentals* stay the same, while the substance of bread is completely changed into the substance of the Lord's body. This unique and wonderful "change the Catholic Church fittingly and accurately calls transubstantiation." ' [25]

By holding to the term 'transubstantiation' and the meaning behind it, it then becomes possible to use other more technical and even less easily understood words, like transfinalisation and transignification, partially to describe what takes place at the consecration.

The first of these words, 'transfinalisation', means that the substance present on the altar at Mass is given (by God) a new purpose. And indeed it is: there is a *new*, different substance present, Christ's body and blood, and clearly it has a new purpose, one different from the purpose of ordinary bread. Unlike the manna of the desert which gave physical nourishment to a particular people for forty years, the Eucharist is destined to nourish all believers, until the end of time, preparing them to become partakers of the divine nature in heaven.

The second of these words, 'transignification', suggests that at Mass the bread and wine are given a new meaning. Not true! That is what Berengarius taught, as we saw earlier, and in doing so he erred. What acquires a new meaning is a new and different substance on the altar, namely, the body and blood of Christ, under the appearances of bread and wine.

In employing these new — or rather, old — concepts we need to be careful not to overemphasise the part of man, to the detriment of the action of God. We do not give a new meaning or purpose to anything; God does, through the power he has bestowed on his priests:

A new purpose because a new substance.

A new meaning and signification because a new substance.

The Catechism of Trent taught in the sixteenth century that Eucharist signifies three things:

(a) *a thing past:* the Passion and Death of our Lord. 'Until the Lord comes, therefore, every time you eat the bread and drink this cup, you are proclaiming his death' (1 Cor 11:26).

(b) *a thing present:* divine and heavenly grace to nuture and preserve the soul. 'Anyone who eats this bread will live for ever' (Jn 6:58).

(c) *a thing future:* eternal joy and glory. 'Anyone who eats my flesh and drinks my blood has eternal life and I shall raise him up on the last day' (Jn 6:54).

Transubstantiation is a unique happening, different from substantial change where one substance becomes another, not yet existing, substance; and from accidental change where only colour, shape and/or other accidents change. In transubstantiation — the production of the body and blood of Christ under the sacramental forms — one substance (bread or wine) becomes an already existing substance (the body and blood of Christ, initially taken from the Virgin Mary and now glorified in heaven), while the accidents (colour, taste etc. of the bread and wine) remain miraculously the same.

The use of the word 'transubstantiation' is important because it guarantees the integrity of our faith in the real presence and in the true sacrificial character of the Mass. It allows us to avoid two extreme and erroneous views: that of imagining Christ's Body and Blood to be present in the Eucharist in a merely natural way (this cannot be so because the observable qualities of bread and wine remain after the consecration) and that of imagining that in no true sense at all is Christ's Body and Blood present in the Eucharist (he *is* present, but sacramentally only).

'Although the species of bread and wine are visible yet we must believe that after consecration the Body and Blood of Christ are alone there'. [26]

CHRIST TOTALLY PRESENT

The usual manner of receiving Holy Communion in the Latin Church is under the one species of bread. In the first millenium Communion under two species was widespread but so too was Communion under one species alone, e.g. the case of those who were ill, or the case of children.

Nowadays in certain cases it is permissible to receive under both species, especially where this way of receiving has 'great importance for the spiritual life of a particular community or group of the faithful and where due reverence for the sacrament is not lessened'. [27] The Holy See has listed out these occasions:

With the bishop's approval and after due instruction the following persons may receive Communion from the chalice:

(1) Newly baptised adults in the Mass following their baptism; newly confirmed adults in the Mass following their confirmation; baptised persons who are being received into full communion with the Church.

(2) The bridegroom and bride at their Nuptial Mass.

(3) The newly ordained at the Ordination Mass.

(4) An abbess in the Mass wherein she is blessed; virgins at the Mass of their consecration; professed religious and their parents, close relatives and other members of their community in the Mass wherein they make their first, renewed or perpetual religious profession on condition that the

profession is made during Mass.

(5) Lay missionaries at the Mass in which they are publicly assigned to their missionary task; others who, during Mass, are entrusted by the Church with some special mission.

(6) A sick person, and all who are present, when Viaticum is given in a Mass lawfully celebrated in the sick person's home.

(7) The deacon and others who have special ministries in a Mass celebrated with singing.

(8) Where there is concelebration:
   (a) all, including laity, who perform a genuine liturgical ministry in the concelebration; and all seminarians who are present,
   (b) all members of institutes professing the evangelical counsels, and other societies whose members dedicate themselves to God by religious vows or promises, provided that the Mass be in their own church or chapel; in addition, all those who live in the houses of these institutes and societies.

(9) Priests who are present at important celebrations and yet are not able personally to celebrate or concelebrate.

(10) All who are making a retreat or some other form of spiritual exercise, in a Mass specially celebrated for those taking part; all who attend a meeting of pastoral commission, in a Mass which they celebrate in common.

(11) Those mentioned in 2 and 4 above, at Masses celebrating their jublilees.

(12) Godparents, parents, spouses and lay catechists of a newly baptised adult, during the Mass of Initiation.

(13) Parents, relatives and special benefactors of a newly ordained priest at his first Mass.

(14) Members of the Community at a Conventual or Community Mass. [28]

However, in all cases the faithful should beforehand be fully conversant with the significance of the rite, namely that the banquet aspect of the Eucharist is more fully manifested and Christ's intention that the new and eternal covenant should be ratified in his Blood is better expressed. [29]

Now, while the Church has always the power to make laws

about the administering of the sacraments, she has no power to alter the nature of the sacraments and for this reason 'the faithful who receive or seek the reception of Communion under both kinds should be thoroughly instructed in the Catholic doctrine about Communion as expounded by the Council of Trent'. [30]

This teaching is that the whole Christ, body and blood, soul and divinity, is present in the Eucharist, under each of the two species and in each and every part of the species, such that, under what to our eyes is only a crumb of bread, the whole Christ is present, and, under what to our eyes is only a drop of wine, the whole Christ is present.

Theologically this is explained as follows: by the words of the consecration the body of Christ is made present under the form of bread and the blood of Christ is made present under the form of wine. But because of the real connection between the body, blood and soul of the living Christ, and because of the Hypostatic Union by which the divine nature is inseparably joined to the humanity, his blood, soul and divinity are present under the species of and his body, soul and divinity are present under the species of wine.

So 'according to the Catholic faith, Christ is received even when people communicate under one kind only. And they are not thereby deprived of any grace necessary for salvation': [31]

'Each (says Saint Augustine), receives Christ the Lord, and he is entire in each portion. He is not diminished by being given to many, but gives himself whole and entire to each'.

It is for this same reason — the presence of the whole Christ in every particle of the sacred Host and in every drop of the previous Blood — the 'one will be careful not to allow any fragment of the host to fall' [32] and 'the greatest diligence and care (should) be taken particularly with regard to the fragments which perhaps fall off the hosts'. [33] In other words the fragments should be gathered up and disposed of in the usual manner, just as the Apostles gathered up twelve baskets of bread which remained after the multitude had satisfied their hunger. Nothing was to go to waste. How much more so then with the Body and Blood of the Lord! Not to do so betrays a weakening faith and a love less than that of the holy women who came on Easter morning at the first sight of dawn, to anoint the dead body of Jesus. Surely what they were willing to do for a dead person we are willing to do for a living one!

Indeed lack of faith, lack of reverence for the Eucharist can have dire consequences, as happened in Corinth where some of those who did not discern the Body of the Lord became infirm and weak, and even died (cf 1 Cor 11:30), presumably as a punishment from God.

PERMANENTLY PRESENT

'If anyone says that after the consecration the body and blood of our Lord Jesus Christ are not present in the marvellous sacrament of the Eucharist, but are present only in the use of the sacrament while it is being received, and not before or after, and that the true body of the Lord does not remain in the consecrated hosts or particles that are kept or are left over after Communion: let him be anathema' [34]

'If anyone says that it is not permissible to keep the sacred Eucharist in a holy place, but that it must necessarily be distributed immediately after the consecration to those who are present; or that it is not permissible to carry the Eucharist respectfully to the sick: let him be anathema.' [35]

The sacrament of the Eucharist is an abiding reality, not a passing action, and this is also unique. The other sacraments exist only at the moment of their administration (although baptism, confirmation and holy orders have a certain permanency about them due to the character they imprint, and so too has matrimony due to its being a stable union). Yet the Blessed Eucharist exists independently of its administration. For this reason it is reserved in the tabernacle and carried in Corpus Christi processions, 'Hidden in the Host he moves through the streets and squares — just as during his earthly life — going to meet those who want to see him, making himself available to those who are not looking for him. And so, once more, he comes among his own people'. [36]

For this reason we are encouraged to spend time in thanksgiving after Communion, using the last minutes of the Mass to good advantage and spending a while in private prayer when Mass has finished. Sometimes the celebrant will include a period of thanksgiving before the Mass finishes. How sad it is to see people lacking in generosity or in awareness in giving time to their God, especially these few precious moments when they are literally a dwelling-place, a tabernacle for the body and blood of the Saviour. 'The sacramental species containing the living body of Christ with his divinity are united to our body by the act of receiving the host. This is indeed a wonderful privilege, and while it lasts, we should not fail to make use of the unique opportunity to speak to our

Lord and our divine lover to thank him, to assure him of our need and love for him, to beg from him the grace to love him more and to live according to his will, and to entreat of him to re-make us and mould us to his heart's desire. If there is any special time for making love to Jesus, certainly it is after receiving Holy Communion as long as his presence remains'. [37]

We are to adore Christ present in the Eucharist with the adoration due to God.

'If anyone says that Christ, the only-begotten Son of God, is not to be adored in the holy sacrament of the Eucharist with the worship of latria, including the external worship, and that the Sacrament, therefore, is not to be honoured with extraordinary festive celebrations nor solemnly carried from place to place in processions according to the praiseworthy universal rite and custom of the holy Church; or that the Sacrament is not to be publicly exposed for the people's adoration, and that those who adore it are idolators: let him be anathema'. [38]

'Nobody eats his flesh without previously adoring it' [39] and the best way of doing this is through paying visits to the Blessed Sacrament and through the age-old custom of Exposition and Benediction of the Blessed Sacrament.

OUTWARD SIGNS OF THE EUCHARIST

The two outward signs of this sacrament are:
   (i)   the matter — bread and wine;
   (ii) the form — the words of consecration.

The bread used is wheaten bread; leavened in the Eastern Church, unleavened in the Western. And 'no one is at liberty on his own private authority, or rather, presumption, to transgress' [40] the law of the Church regarding the kind of bread to be used.

The wine is natural grape wine, to which a few drops of water are added (cf Mk 14:25).

The water signifies three things:

— the water which flowed from the wound opened in the side of Christ by the centurion;

— the human nature of Christ which is hypostatically joined to his divine nature;

— the People of God who are made one with Christ, members of his body.

The aptness of bread and wine as two symbols is easily understood:

(a) those who receive Holy Communion are spiritually nourished by grace in a manner similar to how bread and wine nourish the human mind and body;

(b) as the bread comes from many grains of wheat, and the wine from many individual grapes, so the body of the Church comes from the union of many members, bound together by this sacrament.

And having two distinct material elements, bread and wine, helps us to commemorate and signify in a more lively way the Passion and Death of Jesus in which his blood was separated from his body.

But although there are two elements to this sacrament there is only one sacrament, signifying the one thing, namely the spiritual nourishment whereby we are supported and sustained.

The words of consecration are

(i) for the bread: 'This is my body which shall be given up for you';

(ii) for the wine: 'This is the cup of my blood, the blood of the new and everlasting covenant. It will be shed for you and for all men so that sins may be forgiven.'

When the priest says these words, and only he should say them, for only he has the power of consecration, given in the sacrament of Holy Orders, he must say them with the intention of consecrating, that is to say, he is not simply narrating what Christ did at the Last Supper. He is actually effecting what Christ did on the night he was betrayed.

'The words of Christ complete this sacrament'. [41]

EFFECTS OF THE SACRAMENT

The effects of the sacrament can conveniently be reduced to three:

1. *Union with Christ:* 'The effect which this sacrament has in the soul of a person who receives it worthily, is to unite him with Christ. Since it is by grace that a man is incorporated into Christ and united to Christ's members, it follows that those who receive this sacrament worthily, receive an increase of grace." ' [42]

This union has two aspects to it. It is a sacramental union by which we receive in our bodies the sacrament and become for a short while the dwelling place of the Lord. And it is a permanent spiritual union of love and grace whereby our whole being is incorporated into his Mystical Body and we are joined to him as to our Head. By this union we are enabled to live more and more for God and less and less for ourselves.

By the fact of our union with Christ we are more united to one another for as Saint Paul assures us 'the fact that there is only one bread means that, though there are many of us, we form a single body because we all share in this one bread' (1 Cor 10:17).

2. *Growth in the supernatural life.* 'And all the effects which material food and drink have on the life of our body — maintaining and increasing life, restoring health and bringing pleasure — all these effects this sacrament has on our spiritual life. As Pope Urban says, "in this sacrament we think of our Saviour with gratitude, we are drawn away from evil, we are encouraged to good, and we advance in virtue and in grace." ' [43]

The Eucharist preserves the supernatural life of the soul by giving it the very life of Christ himself, by increasing charity and strengthening the will to resist temptation. It will even remit our venial sins in proportion to the piety and fervour with which we receive it.

3. *Pledge of heaven and future resurrection.* This effect is aptly summed up by the Fathers of the Church: the Eucharist is, says Saint Ignatius of Antioch, 'a means of help toward immortality and an antidote by which one does not die but lives for ever in Jesus Christ'; [44] and, in the words of Saint Irenaeus, 'when our bodies partake of the Eucharist, they are no longer corruptible, as they have the hope of eternal resurrection'. [45]

PREPARATION

The need for preparation goes without saying. Suitable preparation requires that we have faith in the sacrament, distinguishing this heavenly bread from ordinary bread. As soon as children are able to make this distinction they are ready for first Communion.

We ought to be at peace with and sincerely love our neighbour.

If we are conscious of mortal sin not yet confessed and forgiven we may not receive Holy Communion until we have obtained forgiveness in the sacrament of Penance. It is not sufficient, except in cases of urgent necessity which for that very reason only rarely occur, to make an act of perfect contrition before receiving the Eucharist. [46]

We should also be conscious of our unworthiness but this should not deter us from receiving for we will always be un-

worthy. All we need do is acknowledge, with the centurion, that we are not worthy to receive our Lord into our house. 'Go to Communion. It doesn't show lack of respect. Go this very day when you have just got over that "spot of bother". Have you forgotten that Jesus said: "It is not by those who are well, but by those who are sick that the physician is needed." ' [47]
Needless to say to receive the sacrament well we must have the right intention and must believe what the Church teaches about this mystery of faith. For this reason, except in very exceptional circumstances, the Eucharist is not given to non-Catholic Christians (Eastern Orthodox Christians are more readily admitted to the sacrament in cases of need because their faith is the same as ours). [48]

Part of our preparation is to observe the laws of fasting (abstinence from food and alcohol). We should fast for one full hour before receiving; but:

'The period of time of the Eucharistic fast or abstinence from food and alcoholic drink is reduced to approximately one quarter of an hour, for the following: (1) The sick in hospitals or in their own homes, even if they are not confined to bed. (2) The faithful advanced in age who must remain at home because of age or who are living in a home for the aged. (3) Sick priests, even if not confined to bed, and elderly priests, who wish to celebrate Mass or receive Holy Communion. (4) Persons looking after the sick and the aged as well as relatives of the sick and aged wishing to receive Holy Communion with them, whenever they are unable to observe the fast of one hour without inconvenience.' [49]

To drink water or take medicine does not break the Eucharistic fast. We are, however, encouraged to abstain, where possible, from all food and drink from midnight. [50]

How often should we receive the Blessed Sacrament? Every day if at all possible. 'Live in such a manner as to be able to receive every day', says Saint Augustine. [51] And our Lord himself underlined our need to receive him:'Unless you eat the flesh of the Son of Man and drink his blood you cannot have life in you. He that eats my flesh and drinks my blood has everlasting life and I will raise him up on the last day' (Jn 6:53-54).

To help us overcome any tendency to neglect this sacrament the Church obliges us to receive at least once a year, between the beginning of Lent (Ash Wednesday) and the end of Paschal time (Trinity Sunday). The obligation extends to all who have reached the use of reason.

Those who are dying are also obliged to receive the Eucharist if it is possible.

SUMMARY

'At the last Supper on the night he was betrayed, our Saviour instituted the eucharistic sacrifice of his Body and Blood. This he did in order to perpetuate the sacrifice of the Cross throughout the ages until he should come again, and so to entrust to his beloved Spouse, the Church, a memorial of his death and resurrection: a sacrament of love, a sign of unity, a bond of charity, a paschal banquet in which Christ is consumed, the mind is filled with grace, and a pledge of future glory is given to us.' [52]

The Primacy of the Pope in the Church

Pedro Rodriguez

I

THE PRIMACY OF THE POPE AND THE HIERARCHICAL STRUCTURE OF THE CHURCH

The well-known Lutheran scholar W. Pannenberg had this to say when asked about the Papacy: ' Leaving aside for the moment the question whether the papacy is of divine or human right, the need for a ministry of unity in the Church is so evident that negative Protestant attitudes ought no longer be adopted'. [1] The statement on the question of authority in the Church agreed upon by Catholic and Anglican theologians at Venice in 1976 *(Authority in the Church)* acknowledges a 'primatial authority' side by side with a 'conciliar authority'. The document then goes on to affirm that 'the only see which makes any claim to universal primacy and which has exercised and still exercises such *episcope* is the see of Rome, the city where Peter and Paul died. It seems appropriate that in any future union a universal primacy such as has been described should be held by that see.' [2]

These two opinions reflect a state of mind which nowadays is quite widespread among non-Catholic Christians. Looking at things from very different points of view the conclusion is reached that in the Church there must be a world authority which is the source of unity. And it is further seen that in the history of Christianity such authority has only ever been claimed by the Roman Pontiff. Different scholars, some armed with reasons taken from the Bible, others appealing to Tradition, and still others arguing in terms of logical coherence, are coming to the same conclusion, namely, that the papacy has an absolutely necessary role to play at the centre of Christianity.

Obviously many of the statements and stances taken by non-Catholics regarding the papacy only coincide partially with the teaching of the Catholic Church about the power and ministry of Peter's successor. But it is highly significant that, as Dr Pannenberg's parenthesis shows, Catholic dogmatic teaching that the primacy of the Pope belongs, by the will of Christ, to the fundamental structure of the Church is now even being discussed by non-Catholics. The re-consideration of the topic in some sectors of the Anglican and evangelical churches (and the same could be said of the Orthodox churches) is in the sharp contrast with the more usual neglect of the subject altogether. This is not the place to study the historical and spiritual reasons which have given rise to this new interest in the papacy. It suffices to say that they show how much to the point were the words of a recent Catholic convert: 'If God had not instituted the primacy of the Roman Pontiff we men would have had to invent it . . .'

This new openness in Protestant circles is in sharp contrast too to the criticisms levelled by some Catholics at the traditional teaching of the Church. Perhaps as a way of making it easier for our separated brethren to approach Rome one forgets far too frequently what Vatican Council II has said regarding ecumenical dialogue: 'It is essential that the doctrine be clearly presented in its entirety. Nothing is so foreign to the spirit of ecumenism as a false irenicism which harms the purity of Catholic doctrine and obscures its genuine and certain meaning.' [3] Accordingly, it will be useful now to recall some central points of Catholic teaching regarding the authority of the Roman Pontiff, successor of Saint Peter in the primacy of the universal Church.

THE WILL OF GOD REGARDING HIS CHURCH

Pope Leo XIII gave us in his encyclical *Satis cognitum* (1896) a very clear guideline which must be borne in mind when studying the nature and fundamental structure of the Church: 'The origin of the Church and its whole constitution are matters determined by free will. Therefore, any judgement about them must be based on *factual history*, and we should investigate, not the ways in which *it was possible* that there should be only one Church, but how *the founder fixed it* that there could be only one.' [4]

There we have the whole question posed in correct terms. What counts are not more or less brilliant theories about the Church and her organisation but the will of Christ, foundation stone and founder of the Church. In other words, the nature, origin and fundamental structure of the Church are known not by the intellectual skill and wisdom of her pastors and theologians, but by listening humbly to divine revelation — Sacred Scripture and Tradition — which witnesses to the foundational will of Christ. In this way, when the Church explains the mystery of herself and expounds it infallibly as a doctrine of faith she has the most well-founded confidence that all diligent and honest research into the sources of revelation — recognised as the Word of God — carried out by our separated Christian brethren cannot but substantiate the teachings of the Magisterium or, at least, point in the direction of them.

It is to Christ then that we must look and listen. 'This is my beloved Son . . . Listen to him' (Mt 17:5). The guidelines of Pope Leo XIII must, in the words of Vatican Council II, preside over all ecumenical dialogue: 'All are led to examine their own faithfulness to Christ's will for the Church.' [5]

The following words of Pope Paul VI can serve as a short synthesis of the will of Christ for the constitution and make-up of his Church:

Christ promised and sent two elements to constitute his work, to extend in time and over all the world the kingdom founded by him and to make of redeemed mankind his Church, his Mystical Body, in expectation of his second and triumphal return at the end of the world. These elements are the apostolic college and the Spirit. The apostolic college works externally and objectively. It forms, one might say, the material body of the Church and gives her a visible and social structure. The Spirit works internally, within each person and within the community as a whole animating, vivifying and sanctifying. These two agents, namely the apostolic college whose successor is the sacred hierarchy, and the Spirit of Christ, which makes the Church Christ's ordinary instrument in the ministry of the Word and the Sacraments, work together. On Pentecost morning they are seen in a marvellous harmony at the beginning of Christ's great work. [6]

For the remainder of this article we will be concerned with the first of these two elements.

The Catholic Church teaches as a doctrine of faith that Christ gave the Church, in his Apostles, a hierarchical structure of an episcopal nature and that within the hierarchy and the Church he established a primacy of authority in the successor of Saint Peter.

'All the faithful, from the Pope to the child who has just been baptised, share in one and the same vocation, the same faith, the same Spirit, the same grace.' [7] Nonetheless, when it is affirmed that the Church is a hierarchical society we are in substance saying that in spite of 'the radical or fundamental equality' which is to be found among the People of God, the Church has structures, features and differentiations by virtue of which she is a society in which there is a 'functional inequality.' [8] That is to say: not all the faithful have the same function or mission. For this reason Pope Saint Pius X could say that 'the Church is essentially an unequal society, that is, a society composed of two types of people: shepherds and sheep'. [9]

This hierarchical structure is not the result of socio-political influences but stems from the will of Christ. This has been stated solemnly by both the Council of Trent and Vatican I [10] but it is Vatican II which has given a detailed summary:

> The Lord Jesus, having prayed at length to the Father, called to himself those whom he willed and appointed twelve to be with him, whom he might send to preach the kingdom of God (cf Mk 3:13-19; Mt 10:1-42). These apostles (cf Lk 6:13) he constituted in the form of a college or permanent assembly, at the head of which he placed Peter, chosen from among them (cf Jn 21:15-17). He sent them first of all to the children of Israel and then to all peoples (cf Rom 1:16), so that, sharing in his power, they might make all peoples his disciples and sanctify and govern them (cf Mt 28:16-20; Mk 16:15; Lk 24: 45-48; Jn 20:21-23) and thus spread the Church and, administering it under the guidance of the Lord, shepherd it all days until the end of the world (cf Mt 28:20). [11]

Here we have the *hierarchical principle* of the Church established in the persons of the Apostles. The Council goes on to say that this structure, which is of divine origin, is a constitutive part of the Church for all time, not just for the beginnings of the Church but for today as well. This is so, it says, by virtue of the *principle of apostolic succession*. 'That divine mission, which was committed by Christ to the Apostles, is destined to last until the end of the world (cf Mt 28:20), since the Gospel, which they were charged to hand on, is, for the Church, the principle of all its life for all time. For that very reason the Apostles were careful to appoint successors in this hierarchically constituted society.' [12] The Council then explains in great detail, and attentive to historical reality, to 'factual history' in the words of Pope Leo XIII, how this transmission of authority and ministry was made 'to the bishops and their helpers, the priests and deacons'. This whole procedure, we are told, must be related to *the will of Christ:* 'He willed that the successors [of the Apostles], the bishops namely, should be the shepherds in his Church until the end of the world'. [13] And finally, the Council solemnly declares: 'The sacred synod consequently teaches that the bishops have by divine institution taken the place of the Apostles as pastors of the Church, in such wise that whoever despises them despises Christ and him who sent Christ (Lk 10:16).' [14]

'This divinely instituted hierarchy, which is composed of bishops, priests and ministers' [15] received the mission which Christ has entrusted to his Apostles. 'With priests and deacons as helpers, the bishops received the charge of the community, presiding in God's stead over the flock of which they are the shepherds, in that they are teachers of doctrine, ministers of sacred worship and holders of office in government.' [16]

The sacrament of Order is the way established by Christ in perpetuating in his Church this essential hierarchy [17] to which he has given the power of mission with its threefold office of teaching, sanctifying and ruling the faithful. 'The holders of office, who are invested with a sacred power, are, in fact, dedicated to promoting the interests of their brethren so that all who belong to the People of God, and are consequently endowed with true Christian dignity, may, through their free and well-ordered efforts towards a common goal, attain to salvation.' [18]

PRIMACY OF THE ROMAN PONTIFF

The Church's teaching about the authority and ministry of the Pope within the Church places, also by the express will of Christ, that authority and ministry at the very centre of her hierarchical structure. The universal authority of the Roman Pontiff, witnessed to throughout the history of Christianity and proposed as a dogma of faith by the Council of Florence in 1439, [19] was given a detailed dogmatic explanation by Vatican Council I in 1870 in its dogmatic constitution on the Church of Christ *(Pastor aeternus).* This document, in turn, was taken up and confirmed by Vatican II in 1964.

It is interesting to note that, before describing the content of this power and authority, Vatican I wished to underline its *purpose* and *meaning* in the Church according to *the will of Christ.*

This authority exists so that 'the episcopate might be one and un-divided and that the whole multitude of believers might be preser-ved in unity of faith and communion by means of a well-organised priesthood.' [20] 'In order that the episcopate itself might be one and undivided he (Christ) put Peter at the head of the other Apostles, and in him he set up a lasting and visible source and foundation of the unity both of faith and communion.' [21]

Within this basic framework the Church has given her teaching on the primatial authority of the Roman Pontiff in three well defined points: 1. the institution of the primacy in the person of Peter the Apostle; 2. the perpetuity of the primacy through the principle of succession; 3. the nature of this primatial power.

We will now study each of these three points in turn.

1. Institution of the primacy in the person of the Apostle Peter

It is a matter of faith that the blessed Apostle Peter 'was con-stituted by Christ the Lord as the Prince of all the Apostles and the visible head of the whole Church militant' and 'that he rec-eived immediately and directly from Jesus Christ our Lord not only a primacy of honour but a true and proper primacy of jurisdiction.' [22] The Church affirms that this is witnessed to by 'the testimony of the Gospel' [23] and is the 'very clear teaching of the Holy Scriptures.' [24]

The scriptual texts brought forward by the Council are the two following very well-known passages:

(a) the first is known as the 'text of the promise': 'Blessed are you Simon, son of Jonah, because it was not flesh and blood that revealed this to you but my Father who is in heaven. And now I say to you: You are Peter and on this rock I will build my Church and the gates of hell will not prevail against it. I will give you the keys of the kingdom of heaven. Whatever you bind on earth will bound in heaven. And whatever you loose on earth will be loosed in heaven' (Mt 16:16-18);

(b) the second is known as the 'fulfilment text': 'Feed my lambs, feed my sheep' (Jn 21:15ff).

An analysis of other numerous texts of the New Testament would show what precisely was the will of Christ regarding the humble fisherman from Galilee, how Peter afterwards exercised his primacy, and how conscious the other Apostles and the first Christians were that Simon was at the head of the mission which Christ has entrusted to them all. [25]

2. The successor of Peter: perpetuity of the primacy in the Bishop of Rome

As regards this point the dogmatic teaching of Church runs as follows: 'It is according to the institution of Christ our Lord, himself, that is, by divine law, that Saint Peter has perpetual successors in the primacy over the whole Church' and that 'the Roman Pontiff is the successor of Saint Peter in that primacy.' [26]

A. The Principle of Succession

What we saw earlier for the hierarchy of the Church in general we see again but this time applied to the Pope, namely, on the one hand the *principle* of succession as a truth of faith, and, on the other, the *fact* of the succession as it is found in the bishop of Rome. When speaking of the primacy of Peter Vatican I appealed to the texts of Holy Scripture which established it. Now, when speaking of the succession, the Council, and in this it will be followed almost a century later by Vatican II, [27] proceeds not directly from Sacred Scripture but from the principle of indefectibility and perpetuity in the Church. Since by the will of Christ the Church has to last until the end of time, so too must the principle and foundation of unity given by Christ last.

And so theology finds the succession in the primacy of Peter affirmed implicitly in the word of Christ to Simon (Mt 16:16-18 & Jn 21:15ff).

Tradition gives the all important argument, namely the consciousness that the Church has always held that the primacy was preserved in the person of the bishop of Rome. As an example of this Tradition these words spoken by the Pope's legate at the Council of Ephesus in 431 will suffice: 'No one doubts; in fact, it is obvious to all ages that the holy and most Blessed Peter, head and Prince of the Apostles, the pillar of faith, and the foundation of the Catholic Church, received the keys of the kingdom from our Lord Jesus Christ, the saviour and redeemer of the human race. Nor does anyone doubt that the power of forgiving and retaining sins was also given to this same Peter who, in his successors, lives and exercises judgement even to this time and forever.' [28]

As far back as the second century Saint Irenaeus of Lyons, when studying the criteria for sound teaching, had recourse to the apostolic succession and in particular 'to the great church, the oldest and best known of all, founded and established in Rome by the glorious Apostles Peter and Paul . . . all other churches ought to be in agreement with this church because of her more powerful authority . . . for in her is preserved the tradition which comes from the Apostles.' [29]

B. *The succession and the plans of God*

The truth is that it would have been very 'comfortable', from the point of view of theological argumentation, if the text from Saint Matthew which is so often quoted ran along these lines: 'And to you *and your successors* I give the keys of the kingdom of heaven . . .' The same could be said about other important texts on the hierarchical constitution of the Church in general e.g. 'Go, therefore, you *and your successors,* make disciples of all nations . . . as my Father has sent me so I send you and your successors . . .'

But it is easy to see that this way of speaking would be foreign to the way Jesus refers to his work of redemption and to his Church, for he speaks in a prophetic and symbolic way. It has been said, not without a dash of humour, that it is a good thing that the Gospel of Saint Matthew has not named the successors of Saint Peter, for if it had, there would surely be people to see this as one more reason to reject the authenticity of the Gospel itself.

Perhaps the most striking element in the context of this Gospel for understanding the silence of Jesus about the succession in the apostolic college is his constant decision to keep hidden from the Apostles, and from the rest of men, the 'day of the Lord', the parousia, the end point of salvation history whose imminence he always leaves open: 'Stay awake, because you do not know either the day or the hour' (Mt 25:13).

3. *The nature of the Papal Primacy*

Chapter 3 of the dogmatic constitution on the Church of Vatican Council I *(Pastor aeternus)* is the principal document of the Magisterium about the content and nature of the primatial power of the Roman Pontiff. Chapter 4 is a development and defining of one particular characteristic of this primatial power, namely the Pope's supreme teaching authority i.e. when the Pope speaks *ex cathedra* he teaches the doctrine of the faith infallibly. The magisterium of the Roman Pontiff is one of the chief elements of his primatial authority.

(a) *Primacy of jurisdiction:* The primacy spoken about by Vatican I is a primacy of jurisdiction. The word 'jurisdiction' underlines the binding power of the Church. It demands obedience of all the faithful. It is in opposition to a primacy of honour *(primus inter pares)* and to a primacy of direction which might be endowed with the power of advising and guiding, but not with the power of commanding. [30] The word, as is obvious, has its roots in juridical language. But what is defined by the Council transcends juridical categories and can be understood more fully in the light of the properties which the Council assigns to the primatial power of the Pope. [31] The Pope's power is

(i) *universal:* it extends to the whole Church; i.e. to all the members of the Church (pastors and faithful) as to all the various matters which can arise;

(ii) *ordinary:* it is not extraordinary, which would mean that it can be used only in exceptional circumstances; nor is it delegated, that is, it belongs inherently to the office of Pope and is not delegated to him by someone else;

(iii) *supreme:* meaning that it is not subordinated to any other authority; [32]

(iv) *full:* it takes in all questions which might arise in the life of the Church, and does so from every point of view;

(v) *immediate:* it need not be exercised through intermediaries and where necessary can have the most practical applications.

(b) *Bishop of the Catholic Church:* The authority of the Pope is truly episcopal. [33] This feature is very important because it connects the juridical terminology in which the aforementioned properties are expressed, with the sacramental and ministerial meaning which the term *episcope* has in the New Teastament. The Pope is indeed a bishop, and his power has an episcopal character and a pastoral purpose. It is not concerned with human or political matters but is rather a power for fulfilling the three-fold mission of teaching, sanctifying and leading to God the flock of Christ. For this reason Pope Paul VI delighted in calling himself *Bishop of the Catholic Church* and under this title he signed the various documents of Vatican II. Undoubtedly he is bishop of Rome, and not of Dublin or Cologne, but as bishop of Rome he is also Pope, successor of Peter, and has, over all the Church (over all dioceses and all members of the Church), the office which is proper to a bishop. [34]

A study of this truly episcopal power is the simplest way of understanding more deeply the nature of papal authority. The Apostle Peter, he who was charged by Christ with looking after the flock, is he who has the most vivid awareness that his ministry is ' ` be a mere instrument in the hands of Christ, head of the Church. 'The primacy of Peter in leading and serving the Christian people was going to be a pastoral primacy, a primacy of love. The nature and efficacy of the pastoral function of the Apostolic primacy would be based on the undying love of Peter for Jesus'. [35] Accordingly it is Peter who encourages the shepherds of the Church to exercise their ministry with their eyes fixed on Christ, so that 'when the chief shepherd appears you will be given the crown of unfading glory' (1 Pt. 5:4). The work of bishops consists in making it easy for the faithful, and for all men, to turn, not to the shepherds of the Church, but 'to the shepherd and guardian of your souls' (Christ) (1 Pt 2:25).

Christ is the Shepherd; Christ is the Bishop. This is Peter's message because when Jesus promised him the primacy, Peter heard him speak of *my* Church, not *your* Church. All bishops, with Peter at their head, are *vicars,* that is, they take the place of Christ on earth. To enable them to fulfil their mission of service he conferred on them the necessary power.

(c) *Power and service of Peter.* Frequently nowadays, and rightly so, because it is based on Scripture and Tradition, we speak of the mission of the Pope and the bishops as a ministry, as a service. Indeed, they are there to serve. 'The office which the Lord has committed to the pastors of his people is, in the strict sense of the term, a service, which is called very expressively in Sacred Scripture, a *diakonia* or ministry'. [36] One of the titles proper to the Pope himself is 'servant of the servants of God'. The term 'service' cannot be understood as a divesting themselves of the authority which is theirs by right, opposing service to power. That would be a most unbiblical and untraditional way of understanding the word 'ministry'. The Pope and the bishops can only render the Church the service God wants from them if they exercise their power, which is of divine origin and which they, and only they, have. If they were not to use their power, they would be unable to serve; they would be of no use. Now all of us Christians ought to serve one another as Christ loved us and served us. But bishops, besides being counted among the faithful themselves, are pastors and must serve their brethren and children through the use of their pastoral power. Such service demands humility ('The greatest among you must be your servant', Mt 31-11) and fortitude ('The Holy Spirit has made you overseers to feed the Church of God', Act 20:28). Saint Leo the Great, paraphrasing the words of Jesus, puts it like this: 'You are a Rock, Simon. Rather, I am the unshakeable Rock, I am the Cornerstone which unites what was separated. I am the foundation and no one can lay any other. And yet, you Simon, you also are a Rock because I am going to give you my strength, in such a way that, by this sharing, the power which is only mine will be common to you and to me'. [37]

(d) *Unity: reason for the primacy.* Vatican Council I affirmed that the authority of the Pope, and the resulting obligation to obey him, took in 'not only matters that pertain to faith and morals, but also matters that pertain to discipline and government of the Church throughout the whole world'. [38] It is what we call a universal power (applicable, it is clearly understood, to ecclesiastical matters only). The power which the Pope receives from Christ has its own internal statutes and lays upon the successor of Saint Peter a very grave moral obligation.

Earlier on I referred to this service on behalf of the unity of the Church. The Pope has a very wide power in order to be able to serve in a supreme way the unity of the Church. He must use his authority whenever it is required and in the way it is required, so as to serve the unity of faith and communion in the Church. Not to use it could constitute a serious fault; and to hinder its exercise is to hinder the supreme way which Christ has instituted for keeping his Church one.[39] On the other hand, if the Pope were to intervene with his supreme authority where it was not needed he would be making use of the power conferred on him by Christ in a way contrary to the meaning of that power which, in the whole Church, is 'for building up, not pulling down' (2 Cor 10:8) and is 'for us men and for our salvation'. In the ministry of the Pope to build up and to save is to care for the unity of faith and of communion among pastors and faithful.

(e) *The Pope, Vicar of Christ.* The primacy of the Pope is a mystery in the economy of salvation. And to this mystery belong those internal statutes just previously spoken about.

'In his chief ministry the Pope is obliged by the objective rules of faithfulness which derive from the revealed Word of God, from the fundamental constitution of the Church and by Tradition'.[40] He has the necessary divine assistance to carry out his office. But this does not relieve him of a very grave responsibility before Christ whom 'God has appointed to judge everyone, alive and dead' (Act 10:42). It demands of the holder of the office of Bishop of the Catholic Church humility, prudence and holiness and of the faithful continual prayer to God for the head of the Church on earth.

However, and this is all important, on earth there is no external tribunal, neither in the Church nor in civil society to which one can appeal against his decisions. The Pope must look for advice, take the steps which prudence demands in the delicate function of governing the Church, listen to the opinion of his brother bishops, etc.; but 'the judgement of the Apostolic See, whose authority is unsurpassed, is not subject to review by anyone, nor is anyone allowed to pass judgement on its decisions. Therefore, those who say that it is permitted to appeal to an ecumenical council from the decisions of the Roman Pontiff (as to an authority superior to the Roman Pontiff) are far from the straight path of truth'. [41]

We reach here, perhaps, the nerve centre of all the teaching about the primacy. It is what most brings out the fact that we are faced with 'a mystery of faith' and not with 'an organisational factor' in the Church ascertainable by the natural light of human reason. But it also brings us to take our stance on what is the ultimate basis of the whole mystery, a basis which is centered on Christ himself. The basis of the primacy is, on the one hand, its historical institution by Christ, but on the other it is the actual presence *today* of Christ in the primatial acts of the Pope. 'The relation of the primacy to Christ is not only historical-causal, but also actual-causal, for in the actions of the Pope Christ himself acts. In them Christ is present here and now. In the activity of the Pope Christ himself is audible and visible. Of the Pope it can be truly said: *he acts in the person of Christ'*. [42] With theological wisdom Saint Catherine of Siena called the Pope the 'gentle Christ on earth' but at the same time conscious of the moral responsibility of the Pope, she urged him to exercise with fortitude his 'service to unity' in the Church, that is to say, to be faithful to his very important mission.

From the time when Saint Clement of Rome intervened in the affairs of the church of Corinth to re-establish peace in that troubled community, down to our own days with its own contemporary methods for governing the universal Church, the Roman Pontiffs have been the instruments willed by Christ for maintaining unity among bishops and for keeping the multitude of the faithful, that is to say, the Church, in a unity of faith and communion. The ways of exercising the primacy have varied with time, but its substance does not change, for it is immutable. Accordingly, the primacy cannot be watered down in the wake of 'episcopalian' or 'democratic' ideals.

'When the Pope acts in virtue of his office he represents at one and the same time the whole Church and the entire body of bishops. But one cannot deduce from this that he receives his power from the community of believers or from the bishops. On the contrary, he receives it from Christ'. [43] 'The Pope', writes Cardinal Ratzinger, 'is not just someone who speaks in the name of the bishops, a kind of mouthpiece they give themselves and which is there to do their bidding. The Pope is where he is, with a direct responsibility before God, to take the place of the Lord, and to ensure the unity of the word and work of Christ in the same way as Christ gave Peter that same function within the community of the Twelve'. [44]

II

THE MAGISTERIUM OF THE POPE AND THE INFALLIBILITY OF THE CHURCH

Probably the best known — and often the worst understood — characteristic of the papacy in the Church is precisely one connected to the Pope's doctrinal teaching authority (magisterium): the teaching authority of the Pope, when he speaks *'ex cathedra'*, is infallible. As I said before, this is the subject of Chapter Four of Vatican Council I's Constitution *Pastor Aeternus,* on which I have been commenting. [49] The title of this chapter (and this is quite interesting) is 'The infallible teaching authority of the Roman Pontiff'. [50] If we bear those words in mind, much light will be shed on the subject: it is not the person of the Pope that is infallible, but his *magisterium* (under certain conditions, as we shall see). So, when many Protestant and many ill-informed Catholics say 'the Pope is infallible' to put this doctrine in a nutshell, they are going off course. But before considering this characteristic of the Pope's magisterium we must investigate why his teaching authority has importance.

THE MAGISTERIUM OF THE POPE: A SUPREME MAGISTERIUM

Vatican I stressed that 'the supreme power of teaching is also included in the apostolic primacy which the Roman Pontiff, as the successor of Saint Peter, the Prince of the Apostles, holds over the whole Church.' [51] Here we see very clearly the essential prophetic — teaching — dimension of the figure of the Pope and specifically of his apostolic primacy. The fact that the People of God (and even non-Christians), in looking at the Pope, see in him, above all, the one who teaches the Gospel of Christ with complete faithfulness: this perfectly reflects the transcendence which the magisterium of the bishop of Rome has for the Church and all mankind.

The *episcopal* root of his primacy — to which I have already referred — means that we can eminently apply to him what the Council of Trent [52] and later Vatican II say regarding all bishops: that 'among the more important duties of bishops that of preaching the Gospel has pride of place.' [52] This last Council explained this episcopal magisterium exactly and beautifully: 'the bishops are heralds of the faith, who draw new disciples to Christ: they are authentic teachers, that is, teachers endowed with the authority of Christ, who preach the faith to the people assigned to them, the faith which is destined to inform their thinking and direct their conduct: and under the light of the Holy Spirit they make that faith shine forth, drawing from the storehouse of revelation new things and old (cf Mt 13:52); they make it bear fruit and with watchfulness they ward off whatever errors threaten their flock (cf Tim 4:14).' [54] Within the context of this magisterium of the bishops, the outstanding magisterium, as I was saying, is that of one particular bishop, that of Rome. Why? Because to him and only to him did Jesus, the foundation and founder of the Church, speak when he addressed Peter: 'I have prayed for you that your faith may not fail; and when you have turned again, strengthen your brethren' (Lk 22:32). These words of our Lord contain the whole meaning of the preaching of Peter and of his successors; and it is here that we find the core of all the doctrine about infallibility which we are examining.

Earlier we saw how *service to unity* was the whole raison d'etre of the Pope's primatial authority. Now we see how this service expresses itself concretely in the sphere proper to the magisterial function of the Pope. The Pope's preaching has as its object *confirming his brethren in the faith*. All Christians are included here, especially those of us who, by the grace of God, are Catholics. But in a very specific way these brothers are the other bishops in the Catholic Church: the Pope's magisterium is a constant reference point for ensuring the *evangelical quality* of the preaching which each bishop does in his own church. The Pope's preaching has as its purpose (to quote Vatican I) 'that the episcopate might be one and undivided, and that the whole multitude of believers might be preserved in unity of faith and communion by means of a well-organised priesthood. [55]

Therefore, tying up all these loose ends, Vatican II could state that 'bishops who teach in communion with the Roman Pontiff are to be revered by all as witnesses of divine and Catholic truth; the faithful, for their part, are obliged to submit to their bishops' decision, made in the name of Christ, in matters of faith and morals and to adhere to it with a ready and respectful allegiance of mind.' [56] If communion with the magisterium of the Pope is the touchstone for adhesion to the magisterium of the bishops, this adhesion is due in a special and direct way to the authentic magisterium of the Pope, as the same Council says: 'this loyal submission of the will and intellect must be given, in a special way, to the authentic teaching authority of the Roman Pontiff, even when he does not speak *ex cathedra,* in such wise, indeed, that his supreme teaching authority be acknowledged with respect, and sincere assent be given to decisions made by him, conformably with his manifest mind and intention, which is made known principally either by the character of the documents in question, or by the frequency with which a certain doctrine is proposed, or by the manner in which the doctrine is formulated.' [57]

THE INFALLIBILITY OF THE CHURCH

Vatican I has passed into history particularly as the Council which defined papal infallibility. What does this word mean? What is its content? Who is the subject — or who are the subjects — of this prerogative? These are important questions which have concerned theologians throughout the centuries [58] and in recent years have even hit the headlines of newspapers. [59]

I do not intend here go to into aspects which are legitimate subjects for theological research; all I want to do is summarise the Church's own teaching through the magisterium. But, to do this, I must first indicate what the word 'infallibility' means here.

(a) Infallibility, what it is and what it is not

First of all, we are dealing with an infallibility which is *shared* and *relative.* That is what the Declaration *Mysterium Ecclesiae* says: 'God himself, who is absolutely infallible, thus deigned to bestow upon his new people, which is the Church, a certain shared infallibility.' [60] So the Church knows that, in an absolute sense, only God is infallible, just as only God is good, true etc. [61] Therefore, speaking of an infallible Church has always meant infallibility which the Church does not have from within herself but by sharing in the infallibility of God, who gives it to the Church because of his irrevocable faithfulness to the Covenant. [62]

Another point must be made: we must not confuse two concepts: Revelation and infallible assistance. 'Revelation', in its theological sense, is an act of God and only of God, by which he enlightens interiorly the human soul — of the Prophet, of the Apostle — and in regard to which the attitude of the person receiving this revelation is basically one of receiving a truth which, prior to this, he did not know. Infallibility, on the other hand, means being preserved from error; it is the result of an action of God termed 'assistance' by which man — the Pope, the bishops, the universal Church — proposes without error or believes without error the Word of God contained in Revelation. Revelation reached its conclusion in the apostolic era; infallible assistance is a constant dimension of the Church. Thus, Vatican I, speaking of the infallibility of the Pope, declared that 'the Holy Spirit was promised to the successors of Saint Peter not that they might make known new doctrine *by his revelation,* but rather, that *with his assistance* they might religiously guard and faithfully explain the revelation or deposit of faith that was handed down through the Apostles.' [63]   And Vatican II put this more exactly when it said, in dealing with the magisterium of the Pope, and of the bishops, that it 'is not superior to the Word of God but is its servant. It teaches only what has been handed on to it. At the divine command and with the help of the Holy Spirit, it listens to this devotedly, guards it with dedication and expounds it faithfully. All that it proposes for belief as being divinely revealed is drawn from this single deposit of faith.' [64]

Another important nuance: when we speak of the infallibility of the Church, this does not mean that the Church has a *perfect* knowledge of divine things, of Revelation, nor that the formulation of the definitions of faith are exhaustive. This is one of the most common mistakes made in this subject: identifying infallibility with perfect knowledge. If understood in that sense only God's own knowledge of the truth is infallible. We are not referring to this when we speak of the Church's infallibility. This means that the Church has an infallibly *true* knowledge of divine Revelation, but not a *perfect* one. The Church indeed has always related her doctrine on infallibility to the state proper to human knowledge here on earth, of which Saint Paul spoke: [65] here we can attain only knowledge of the mysteries of God which is true and valid but at the same time limited, precarious and imperfect. In fact, the Church has defined that in statements about God which take created things as their starting point no similarity can be found so great but that the dissimilarity is even greater than the resemblance. [66] To sum up, what infallibility assures is *certainty* of the truth, compatible with *imperfect knowledge* of the truth.

We could say that the specific content of infallibility — as the very word suggests — is *preservatio ab errore,* preservation from error. That was how the Relator, Monsignor Gasser, explained it to the Fathers of Vatican I: he said that the dogma which would be proclaimed meant that the Pope, by virtue of infallibility and under certain specific conditions, 'cannot err'; [67] and the text of *Pastor Aeternus* in fact based the dogma on the words 'that your faith may not fail' of Luke 22:32, in virtue of which 'the See of Peter always remains untainted by any error.' [68]

From this it follows that the charism of infallibility has a negative content: it excludes error. Its positive content — deep understanding of revealed truth — is the result of the response of the faithful to divine graces (whether normal or exceptional); and in the case of the pastors — the Pope and the bishops — it derives from their effort to study, by all the means at their disposal, Sacred Scripture and the Tradition of the Church, and from their humble docility to the assistance of the Holy Spirit, which they *habitually* have (not only *ad casum,* as in the case of infallible assistance) by virtue of their pastoral mission. Precisely because of this, even infallible definitions — while remaining definitive and irreformable — can be the object of later improvement. Since they do not contain error they are true, infallibly true, for error is the opposite of truth. But a truth can be gone into more; it can be filled out, and expressed better. This is the basis of progress in and development of dogma.

(b) Who in the Church is infallible?

When the Vatican I Fathers were given the draft text, the Relator, Monsignor Zinelli, introduced the subject in this way: 'one thing is quite certain — the infallibility of the Church. This is a dogma of faith. Indeed it is the basic dogma, for we believe all other dogmas by basing ourselves on the authority of the Church (. . .) It is a question, therefore, of defining whether the Roman Pontiff has the same infallibility, and whether he has it in the same specific sense as we know this dogma to have (. . .) Since we have two truths — one admitted by all Catholics as a dogma of faith, and the other which is as yet undefined — we must proceed from the better known to the less well known. Therefore, if we define that the infallibility proper to the Pope is the same as that proper to the Church, we have arrived at the goal we set out to reach'. [69] And so the Council's famous dogmatic definition reads in this way: 'We define as a dogma of faith: that the Roman Pontiff (. . .) enjoys the same infallibility as that with which the divine Redeemer (. . .) wished his Church to be endowed.' [70]

We can see then that in Vatican I it was a truth of faith (before defining the particular infallibility of the Pope) that *the Church* was infallible. Who is this infallible Church? Vatican I, due to certain historical events, [71] was not able to go into this question, though the following draft text had been prepared which fully answered the question: 'This wonderful divine gift, through which the Church of the living God is the pillar and the ground of truth, consists in this: that neither the whole body of the faithful *when believing* nor those who have the task of teaching the whole Church *when exercising that magisterium* can fall into error. Therefore, this should be held as, being infallibily true: a) what is *believed* or what is *taught* in the whole world under the authority of the bishops in communion with the Apostolic See; b) what the bishops themselves teach with the confirmation of the Roman Pontiff, and c) what the Roman Pontiff himself, speaking *ex cathedra,* defines as something to be believed or taught.' [72]

Analysis of this fine text helps us understand who is this infallible Church according to the mind of the Fathers of Vatican I. 'The universal Church', said Saint Thomas Aquinas, 'cannot err, because it is governed by the Holy Spirit, who is the Spirit of the Truth'. [73] The Church endowed with infallibility is, then, the universal Church, for, according to unanimous tradition, *fidei non potest subesse falsum,* [74] the faith cannot fall into error. But this universal Church, as we have seen, expresses this gift of infallibility on three levels:

(1)   First in the teaching — *in docendo* — of the totality of the hierarchial magisterium, in communion with and subordinated to the bishop of Rome, successor of Peter, that is to say, when the episcopal college gives its maximum doctrinal authority to statements regarding the meaning and interpretation of the truths entrusted to the Church.

(2)   Then, in the *ex cathedra* definitions of the Roman Pontiff, that is, when his supreme magisterium verifies the conditions implied by that expression.

(3) Finally, in the act of faith of the *'congregatio fidelium'* that is, the assembly of the faithful *in credendo,* when they make the act of divine and catholic faith by which they adhere to revealed doctrine as preached by the magisterium of the Church. [75]

To put it schematically:

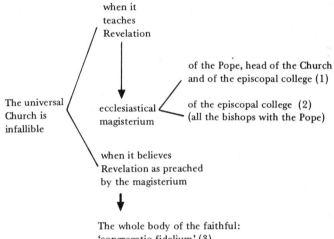

Only the first point — papal infalliblity — was dealt with by Vatican I. It fell to Vatican II, almost one hundred years later, to deal with the doctrine of points 2 and 3 — the infallibility of the episcopal college when it teaches, and the infallibility of the universal Church when it believes. What the Vatican I Fathers used as their point of departure was gone into in depth by Vatican II.

Let us look first at the infallibility of the Pope and then see what happened at Vatican II.

THE MAGISTERIUM OF THE POPE, AN INFALLIBLE MAGISTERIUM

The Pope enjoys, *in his magisterium,* the same infallibility as Christ wished his Church to have. This, as we have seen, is the core of the dogmatic definition of Vatican I. But, when making this solemn declaration, the Council added certain important qualifications:

these must be taken into account when trying to understand better what the Church's doctrine on this subject really is. We will look at them, following the same order as they occur in *Pastor Aeternus*.

(a) When is the magisterium of the Pope infallible?

When he speaks *'ex cathedra'*, the Council says. The technical expression refers to the formal act of the Apostle Peter and his successors precisely in so far as they are the teachers who speak from the chair. But the Council gives additional light as to the meaning of the phrase *ex cathedra*.[76] The Pope is infallible in his magisterium when *in defining a doctrine* these four conditions are verified:

(1)   that he is teaching 'in the office of shepherd and teacher of all Christians'; therefore, he is not infallible when he speaks to particular groups, or as a private teacher i.e. as a theologian making observations.

(2)   that he is using 'his supreme apostolic authority' i.e. that he desires to use to its fullest extent his succession to the Apostle Peter's prophetic role: obviously he is not infallible when, although acting as pastor and teacher of all Christians, his magisterium is simply exhortative or addressed to people to encourage them to reflect.

(3)   that he is dealing with 'doctrine concerning faith or morals' says the Council. Michael Schmaus comments: [77] 'the sphere of papal infallibility covers all Revelation and therefore all revealed doctrines dealing with faith and morals, and also the surrounding areas which are so closely related to Revelation that the latter would not be safe if the former were in any way at risk'. This brings in the very important area of natural law, which indicates the kind of behaviour human dignity calls for: if people did not conform to natural law they would not be able to live up to the requirements of the Gospel.

(4)   that this doctrine be proposed 'to be held by the whole Church': here it is clearly referring to the intention the Pope should have of dogmatically *defining* a doctrine i.e. requiring of the whole Church a definitive assent to the doctrine being proposed to it; as Vatican II puts it 'he proclaims (it) in an absolute decision.' [78]

Thus, it is clear that the conditions for an *ex cathedra* definition are very strict: to such an extent that, according to the unanimous opinion of theologians, from 18 July 1870 when Vatican I made this definition up to our own time, only once were they verified: when Pope Pius XII defined the Assumption of our Lady into heaven (1950). But this deeper understanding of the infallible nature of certain acts of the Pope's magisterium has acted as a light and a call to listen with re-doubled attention to his ordinary magisterium also — even though it may not be infallible (apart from the fact that much of the content of this ordinary magisterium must in fact be infallible for other reasons — since it is the universal and constant magisterium of the Church).

(b) How, then, is this magisterium infallible?

Vatican I replies: 'through the divine assistance promised to him in the person of St Peter'. [79] And Vatican II: because these definitions are 'made with the assistance of the Holy Spirit promised to him [the Pope] in the person of blessed Peter himself'.[80] The Pope enjoys *personally* the 'charism of divine assistance' through which the Holy Spirit assures the Church that *what is defined* by the Pope *ex cathedra* is infallible truth. The charism is in the *subject* (the Pope) but the infallibility is in *the doctrine* (the definitions). The basis of papal infallibility is, then, pneumatological (a charism of the Spirit) and it is christological: Christ's infallible prayer ('I have prayed for you'), whose infalliblity is expressed precisely in the sending of the Spirit of Truth (Jn 16: 13) — the 'Spirit of Christ', who is the Truth (Jn 14:6 — who 'assists' him through this charism.

(c) Consequences of the Pope's infallibility

The most notable consequence of this infallibility was defined by Vatican I: 'such definitions of the Roman Pontiff are therefore irreformable because of their very nature *(ex sese)* and not because of the agreement of the Church.' [81] This statement was very badly understood; some thought that it was stating that the Pope could act capriciously and arbitrarily, unconnected with the rest of the Church. In response to this unfair imputation, Catholic theologians proceeded to explain very clearly the meaning of these words. [82] But perhaps the most authoritative interpretation is that given by Vatican II: the cause of their 'being irreformable by their very nature and not by reason of the assent of the Church is, it says, the *charism* of the assistance of the Holy Spirit'. And Christ does not give the Holy Spirit to his Church to legitimise the caprice and prejudices of men, but quite the contrary: to confirm the faith of the brethren, to serve docilely the word of God contained in Holy Scripture and Apostolic Tradition. So part of the internal structure of papal service to the faith (which is rendered possible and is required by the charism which we are discussing) is a most refined relationship, on the Pope's part, with his brothers in the episcopate and with the supernatural sense of the faith of the whole People of God. But what the Pope defines, he defines moved by the Spirit, and in the name of Christ; these definitions, the Council says, oblige all: 'they are in no way in need of the approval of others, and do not admit of appeal to any other tribunal.' [83]

These words of Vatican II are the authentic interpretation of Vatican I's formula. It goes on to say: 'For in such a case the Roman Pontiff does not utter a pronouncement as a private person, but rather does he expound and defend the teaching of the Catholic faith as the supreme teacher of the universal Church, in whom the Church's charism of infallibility is present in a singular way.'

Thus, the Pope's word is not only binding and obligatory for all; it is more than that: it is an event of grace, a calling from Christ through his Spirit; it is a gift of and presence of the Spirit in the whole Church.

4. The infallible magisterium of the episcopal college and the infallible faith for the universal Church

I want now to say a few words on the infallibility of the college of bishops when they teach, and the infallible faith of the faithful taken as a whole: this will conclude my references to the work of Vatican II on this whole subject.

Regarding the college of bishops the Constitution *Lumen Gentium* says: 'Although the bishops, taken individually, do not enjoy the privilege of infallibility, they do, however, proclaim infallibly on the following conditions: namely, when even though dispersed throughout the world but preserving for all that among themselves the bond of communion, in their authoritative teaching concerning matters of faith and morals, they are in agreement that a particular teaching is to be held definitively and absolutely. This is more clearly the case when, assembled in an ecumenical council, they are, for the universal church, teachers of and judges in matters of faith and morals, whose decisions must be adhered to with the loyal and obedient assent of faith'.[84] Further on it stresses again that 'the infallibility promised to the Church is also present in the body of bishops when, together with Peter's successor, they exercise the supreme teaching office.' [85]

The infallibility of the Church *in credendo*, in believing, is gone into in a very important section of the chapter of *Lumen Gentium* devoted to the People of God. The document is explaining how 'the holy People of God shares in Christ's prophetic office' [86] and the key statement is this: 'The whole body of the faithful who have an anointing that comes from the Holy One (cf 1 Jn. 2:20 and 27) cannot err in matters of belief *(in credendo falli nequit)*. This characteristic is shown in the supernatural appreciation of the faith *(sensus fidei)* of the whole people, when, "from the bishops to the last of the faithful" they manifest a universal consent in matters of faith and morals.' [87] A characteristic feature of this infallibility of the Church in its believing is that it is to be found precisely in adhering to and allowing oneself to be guided 'by the sacred teaching authority *(magisterium)* and obeying it (in this way receiving) not the mere word of men, but truly the word of God.' [88]

If one meditates on and explores these three distinct forms in which infallibility is to be found in the Church, with the relations which they imply between Pope and bishops; pastors and faithful; teaching and faith, on the one hand; and on the other between God one and three — the Father, the Son and the Holy Spirit proceeding from them both — and the Church and each one of the faithful, who have the anointing of the Holy Spirit, we will be led even more to wonder at and love the mystery of the Church, which is a mystery of communion. All the structure of the infallibility of the Church in its teaching and in its act of believing is by divine institution at the service of that reality which Saint John expressed in these words: 'Something which has existed from the beginning, that we have heard, and we have seen with our own eyes; that we have watched and touched with our hands; the Word, who is life: this is our subject. That life was made visible: we saw it and we are giving our testimony, telling you of the eternal life which was with the Father and has been made visible to us. What we have seen and heard we are telling you so that you too may be in union with us, as we are in union with the Father and with his Son Jesus Christ. We are writing this to you to make our own joy complete' (1 Jn 1:1-4).

CONCLUSION

THE UNITY OF CHRISTIANS AROUND THE POPE

Paul VI said on one occasion that he saw 'the charism of primacy given by Christ himself in the Church to Peter whose humble but true successor we are, more as a requirement to exercise it than as a right to exercise it.' [89]   To this approach Christians ought to have an attitude such as Monsignor Escrivá de Balaguer described: 'Acting no longer as subjects of authority but with the piety of children, with the affection of those who feel themselves to be and in fact are members of the Body of Christ.' [90] Behind this spirituality of love for the Pope is the deep conviction that he possesses an authority which has no substitute: 'Never tire of preaching love and obedience to the Holy Father. If his figure had not been instituted by Jesus Christ, my mind tells me that a strong central authority — the Holy See — is necessary for helping people see reason who cannot manage to reach agreement, within the Church, and who lost their way spreading error. But over and above these logical reasons is the will of God who has wanted to have a vicar on earth and to assist him infallibly through his Spirit.' [91]

'If our apostolic office,' Paul VI said to the Fathers of Vatican II, 'obliges us to take precautions, to define terms, to prescribe formulas, to indicate the ways in which the bishop's role should be performed, this is — as you well know — with a view to the good of the whole Church and to the unity of the Church, which has a greater need of central direction the more widespread its catholic unity becomes, the graver the dangers and the more urgent the needs of the Christian people in the diverse circumstances of history and, we might add, the more effective the means of social communication become.' [92]

Pope John Paul II acted in a way which we could say is a paradigm of the exercise of the primacy as a service to the unity of the Church, in convoking and holding a special synod of the Church in Holland; this took place in Rome in 1980 under the presidency of the Holy Father and with the participation of all the Dutch bishops and of other prelates and cardinals. 'This synodal assembly', he said at the opening of the synod, 'in which the bishops of the Dutch ecclesiastical province meet together with the bishop of Rome is an unprecedented event. We are all aware of this fact.' [93]
In Holland, as we know, there have been difficulties in connection with unity in the faith and with communion within the Catholic community and between the bishops themselves. The Holy Father' intervention has allowed the bishops to face up to their specific problems, beginning with that of their own communion (among themselves and with the bishop of Rome). The final document, signed by all those taking part and approved by the Pope, is a moving testimony to that *communio pastorum* (communion of shepherds) rediscovered actively in the company of Peter's successor.

Behind the theology on the successor of Peter there is always communion — the unity of the Church in the midst of variety. That is its formal reason, according to divine Revelation: to be the permanent and visible centre and ground of the *communio Ecclesiarum* (communion of churches) which the Spirit of Christ vivifies. In an atmosphere of a crisis of faith and unity this is what many who are not within Peter's ship are sensing. Those of us who by God's grace are in that ship have a serious responsibility not to defraud their hope.

On the Assumption of our Lady

Eamon Sweeney

It might be a surprise to someone reading an article on the Assumption of Mary, body and soul, into heaven to find no mention of Lourdes or Fatima, even though the Mother of God appeared and spoke with people in both of these places. These are what are called private revelations. Even if they become universally known, and even if they are given a feast of their own in the Church's yearly cycle, they can never serve as a source for the teaching of the Church on a particular matter. That teaching must be drawn from the public revelation made by God, which reached its fullest expression in Christ and ended with the death of the last of the Apostles. It is from this source that the Church draws the supernatural truth she teaches when she solemnly declares and defines that Christ took his mother to be with him in heaven when the time came for her life on earth to end. It is the purpose of this article to outline what lies behind the moment 'preordained in the plan of divine Providence', 1 November 1950, when Pope Pius XII defined our Lady's Assumption as a dogma of the Catholic faith. The solemn definition was effected by an Apostolic Constitution titled, as is the custom, by its first words in Latin: *Munificentissimus Deus (The God of all generosity)*. Extensive use has been made of this document in the preparation of what follows though only direct quotations will be referenced.

The fact of the Assumption, which the dogma formally proposes for our acceptance with supernatural faith, makes known to us the depths of Christ's love for his Mother. It shows us her high dignity which God saw fit to crown with this privilege, the finishing touch, almost, of her other privileges. We cannot consider the mystery, however, without also being struck by the manner in which God has manifested it to us. Our coming into possession of the Assumption as a dogma of faith is deeply linked to the mystery of the Church itself as God's instrument to preserve and transmit all that he himself has revealed for our salvation. In order to say why it is that we believe in the Assumption, it will be necessary and also enlightening to examine the question from two points of view. There are first of all the theological arguments which support and explain to some degree the fittingness or suitability of the Assumption — and these must have their place. But it is not because of these that the dogma is defined. I will deal with them, but after arriving at the definition by the other path, which conclusively proves that the Assumption is contained among those supernatural truths that God has revealed.

THE POPE DEFINES

The content of the Catholic faith is established by God. It is full of supernatural truth, but there is great variety in the manner in which God has communicated that truth to us. The message of salvation includes words and deeds. In its transmission by the Apostles, not only did the inspired Scriptures play their role but so did the spoken word of the Apostles themselves, the example they gave and the institutions they established in the early Church. [2] The task of authentically interpreting the truth of the faith is entrusted to the living Teaching Authority of the Church, which guards and expounds it in every age until the end of time.

The Pope, as successor of Saint Peter, is the supreme teacher of the whole Church, and the Church's charism of infallibility is present in him in a singular way when he teaches absolutely and solemnly a doctrine pertaining to faith and morals. Papal definitions — like that of the Assumption — are not new revelation nor new inspiration but definitions in conformity with what has been handed down from apostolic times.

Not all the truth contained in divine revelation is dogma, but only that which is solemnly declared by the Church to be divinely revealed. Much of the Gospel — taking the term in its broad meaning of the good news of the salvation worked by God through Christ — is clear and explicit. There is only need for definition by the teaching authority if some clear point is put in doubt by heresy. That heresy should occur is to be expected, since the truth contained in the words and deeds by which divine revelation is given to us is supernatural, and the words and deeds are capable of varying human interpretation. We must look to the teaching of the Church for their authentic meaning.

The need to defend the faith leads to the definition of dogmas even in relation to explicit parts of divine revelation. Definitions also are made when there are some equally revealed but less obvious truths which are worthy of being formally proposed for acceptance by the members of the Church. In the latter cases the motives that would prompt the making of dogma would not so much be the defence of the faith as the further glory of God and the good of the Christian people.

Pope Pius XII felt that, as well as being to God's glory and to our Lady's honour, the definition of the Assumption of Mary as a dogma would bring many good things to the Church. In the first place, the proclamation of her Assumption would stir up more fervent devotion and love for the Mother of Christ. It would also be a beacon inviting the non-Catholic Christians — especially the Eastern Orthodox churches, which maintain strong devotion to the Mother of God — to share the unity of the Mystical Body in the Catholic Church. For the world at large he hoped that the truth of the Assumption would highlight the value of a life of complete dedication to the service of God as well as the high destiny to which God has called the soul and body of each human being. [3]

To these motives of perennial applicability can be added the empirical one of the constant petitions that had been reaching the Holy See since 1870. It is estimated that between the end of Vatican Council I and the year 1950 over four hundred bishops, some eighty thousand priests and religious and more than eight million lay people from all over the world had formally signed requests that the Assumption be defined as a dogma of the faith.

The proposal of a new dogma of faith is one of those moments in the life of members of the faithful when they are bound to make an explicit internal act of faith. When God speaks, he does so in order that men may hear what he has to say and hold to it by faith. When the Pope defines a dogma like the Assumption of our Lady, body and soul, into heaven, the definition includes the words ' . . . a dogma revealed by God . . . '. To this solemn declaration of divine truth, the response is a formal act of faith.

THE DEPOSIT OF FAITH

The dogmas of the Church are drawn from the deposit of faith. 'Sacred Tradition and Sacred Scripture make up a single sacred deposit of the Word of God, entrusted to the Church.' [4] In it are to be found 'everything that serves to make the People of God live their lives in holiness and increase their faith.' [5] What God has entrusted to the Church is not a dead thing, a relic of times past to be continually polished. It is the Word of God and it is therefore always living and active.

Vatican Council II describes how, under the guidance of the Holy Spirit, progress is made: 'There is growth in insight into the realities and words that are being passed on'. [6] This is precisely how the Church advanced to the point of making the Assumption of our Lady a dogma of faith. Among the words and realities that the Church transmits there is an important part which relates to the mysteries of the life of Mary. Some of these truths of faith about our Lady are quite explicitly found in the deposit, others are less explicit, more are quite hidden. As the Church grew in its understanding of the mysteries with the assistance of the Spirit of Truth, it came to distinguish the Assumption of Mary as being implicitly present in the other revealed mysteries.

'This growth comes about in various ways. It comes through the contemplation and study of believers who ponder these things in their hearts (cf Lk 2:19 and 51). It comes from the intimate sense of spiritual realities which they experience. And it comes from the preaching of those who have received, along with their right of succession in the episcopate, the sure charism of truth'. [7] Each of these three ways has made its own contribution to the development of the dogma of the Assumption, as we shall see.

LOVE GIVES KNOWLEDGE OF THE TRUTH

The philosophers tell us that truth is first of all in things themselves. Then it is in our knowledge of them. We know the truth about something when what we say of it corresponds to what it is in fact. If we know more of the truth of it we can say more of what it is. Some truth can be discovered by man using the powers of his mind that are given him by God. This truth is called natural truth because it has to do with the natural order of things created by God. It is not the whole of truth, however. Above it is another order of truth which is known only to God and in part to the angels and saints. This is the supernatural order and it is completely beyond the power of man's intellect to reach without a supernatural help from God.

God's gift of faith makes us capable of receiving and accepting the supernatural truth contained in the words and works by which God's revelation is communicated to us. Our minds are raised to a new level. Without ceasing to be human we become sharers in the knowledge of God and the saints. The gift of faith is often compared to a light. The quality of light is that it shows things to the eye. The light of faith shows the articles of faith to the eye of the mind as truths believable and to be believed as coming from God. By faith we adhere firmly to the truths of faith although their intrinsic truth is not evident to our natural minds. When a person is strong in the faith, the gift of faith gives him a certain ease of distinguishing what is to be believed and what is not. When believers contemplate the truths they hold in faith and study the inter-relationships that exist between the mysteries of the faith, and how the mysteries are connected with the last end of man, they grow in insight into them. The constant meditation and contemplation of the truths about the Mother of God and the harmony which exists between them led generations of faithful Christians to *see* with the light of faith that the Assumption is present in the deposit of faith.

The study of the faith is not something could or lifeless. *Verbum spirans amorem* is a phrase that Saint Augustine applied to Christ. He is a Word breathing forth Love, who must be received with love. The word of God contained in the deposit of faith also calls for a loving reception from the believer. The contemplation of Christians is a contemplation in love of the revealed mysteries and especially of those mysteries that tell us of God's intimate plans relating to the life of Mary. 'The fire of love brings us to knowledge of the truth,' [8] says Saint Thomas Aquinas. Love for Mary, who is Mother of God and our mother too, enabled Christians down through the centuries to ever more clearly contemplate the privileges of our Lady as a harmonious whole in which the Assumption occupied its rightful place.

Faith that contemplates in charity is further assisted by the gifts of the Holy Spirit. The highest of these gifts is wisdom, which is the special accompaniment of charity. Through this gift, the believer is enabled to judge rightly about supernatural matters by a kind of kinship or co-naturalness with them. He has a sort of 'taste' or 'feeling' for supernatural truth. It is no coincidence that the word for 'wisdom' in Latin, *sapientia,* comes from the verb *sapere,* which means 'to have taste' as well as 'to be wise.' Through his gifts the Holy Spirit brings about growth in insight among the faithful, even the formally uneducated, through the intimate sense of spiritual realities that they experience. We owe the remarkable unanimity that existed in the Church at all levels and among all types of people that Mary was taken up into heaven body and soul to the constant work of the Holy Spirit filling the hearts of the faithful.

The great Basilica of St Peter's in Rome is an eloquent testimony of how Christians revered and honoured the tombs of those who had been close to Christ. His simple grave on the Vatican Hill was carefully noted and, in the measure that the troubled times of persecution allowed, gradually given more honour. Improvement succeeded improvement until the grave of the fisherman from Galilee became the imposing monument we see today.

Yet, it does not seem at all strange to us that no like occurence is to be found in relation to our Lady. Could the location of her grave — had she been laid in it — have been forgotten? Would not her remains have been precious relics and her resting place have become a famous attraction for pilgrims? The only explanation for the fact that the Church never sought or exposed to public veneration the remains of the Blessed Virgin is that in the heart of Christians there lay the intimate conviction that Mary was elsewhere. Saint Bernardine of Siena called this argument 'a tangible proof' of the Assumption.

DEATH OR DORMITION?

Even though there is no tomb of Mary, there are on the other hand many churches dedicated to the Blessed Virgin received into heaven. These often have the title of the *transitus* (passage) of Mary or of her *dormitio* (sleep). It was under these titles that the liturgy of the Church honoured God in the mystery of the Assumption in the earliest days of the development of the dogma.

Did Mary's soul leave her body, even if only for a short time before both body and soul were taken into heaven? If this is the case, then our Lady died, for death is the separation of soul and body. Or did she simply have a blessed sleep (dormition) at a certain moment set by God's providence until she was 'wakened' by her Son as he brought her to the heavenly home? Pope Pius XII deliberately refrained from deciding this question when he made the solemn definition of the dogma. He used the phrase 'at the end of her earthly life' in order to leave either possibility to the prayerful judgement of believers, subject as always to further possible authoritative decisions by the Teaching Authority.

The choice between holding that our Lady actually died before being assumed and that she was assumed during a final sleep depends on what one thinks will give more honour to God and to

Mary. Those who favour the view that Mary did die usually do so because they see in her death a more complete union of the Mother with the Son who by his death on the Cross redeemed us from our sins. There can, of course, be no implication in this that while Mary was dead (a state which would have necessarily lasted only a brief time) her body suffered any decay at all. It is the content of the dogma that being assumed body and soul into heaven Mary never bore any of the penalty of original sin which is the decay of the body in the grave.

There are perfectly sound reasons for taking the view that the Mother of God died, but perhaps here again it is only love that can give us the right direction. Christ achieved complete victory over our death in his own death and resurrection. Mary was already fully associated with that death as she stood beside the Cross, her soul pierced with sorrow as Simon had prophesised. When we consider that the Assumption is due to the Son's love for his Mother, it is hard to see why he should withhold from her in any way the victory over death he had fully obtained and in which she had cooperated most intimately.

Pope John Paul II says in a homily:

If, in fact, 'those who belong to Christ' 'will be made alive' 'at his coming', then it is correct and understandable that his sharing in the victory over death should be experienced first precisely by her, his Mother; she who is 'of Chirst' in the most complete way. (. . .) She who in her human conception was Immaculate — that is, free from sin, whose consequence is death — for that very fact, should she not be free from death, which is the consequence of sin? That 'coming' of Christ spoken of by the Apostle (. . .), should it not perhaps take place, in just this one case, in an exceptional way, so to speak immediately, that is, at the moment of the conclusion of earthly life? (. . .) Therefore that end of life, which for all men is death, in Mary's case Tradition correctly prefers to call a 'sleeping.' [9]

More and more people who love our Lady speak of her 'leaving this life' rather than 'dying'. But we have jumped from the most human of indications for the Assumption, that is, the absence of a burial place, to the limits of what has been defined as of Faith. We must now see how the Church knows that the dogma of the Assumption is divinely revealed.

In a famous phrase from the letter to the Hebrews, Saint Paul tells us that 'faith is the substance of things to be hoped for; it is the evidence of things unseen'. [10] This inspired definition tells us two quite important things about the supernatural virtue. First, faith constitutes a real link between God and man, which, if persevered in with charity, will lead a person to achieve fulfillment of what it promises. Thus, it is the 'substance', the core, as it were, of our ultimate union with God in heaven. Our link with God through the gift of faith is made through acceptance of God's word on matters that we are unable to see with our own mind. By accepting his Revelation we 'cling' to God in a manner analogous to a person clinging to his own opinions. Through faith we come to know things that are unknown and indeed unknowable for us. Faith gives such firmness that the truths almost seem evident, though in reality they are hidden. Faith is the evidence of things unseen.

If we are to hold unseen things by faith, God must reveal them to us. This is true of everything we believe with supernatural faith and especially true of the most supernatural truths. Two examples of principal supernatural truths will help to clarify this point. The resurrection of Christ is a historically verifiable event. The empty tomb, the shroud, the human factors that make it totally impossible that there was any attempt to steal Christ's body, all of these point to the resurrection as a fact. They cannot however tell us what the resurrection means or what is the state of Christ's humanity once he is risen. This supernatural content of the event had to be made known, firstly by Christ himself during his conversations with the Apostles during his public life, then by the angels at the tomb and finally by Christ now risen from the dead and appearing to his Apostles in the course of forty days. Something similar happens at the ascension. The Apostles see Christ lifted up to the sky until he is removed from their sight by a cloud. They have the evidence of their eyes for his departure. But, what of his arrival in heaven? They cannot know that he has gone definitively to heaven and will not come again until he is to judge the world unless they are told it. They are in fact told it by the angels who appear to them while they are still looking upwards. As in the case of the resurrection, the supernatural content of the events had to be revealed.

An old tradition holds that the Apostles were present at Mary's passing. If they or other witnesses saw her leave this earth, we have no record of it. Even to have seen her leave would not be enough to establish the Assumption as a matter of supernatural faith unless there was some supernatural revelation of the supernatural terminus to which our Lady was brought. If her going and her destination had been recorded in inspired Scripture, that would be enough. But it is not mentioned at all in the Old or New Testament. It has been revealed by another means.

THE 'SENSUS FIDEI'

The Church does not create the content of the faith but believes what its Teaching Authority proposes to it as being divinely revealed. The source from which the Teaching Authority draws its teaching is Sacred Scripture and Sacred Tradition. In determining the content of Sacred Tradition the Church can make use of what the Second Vatican Council called the *sensus fidei*. This not easily translated phrase refers to the fact that the Church is maintained in the unity of the faith and makes progress in it through the influence of the Holy Spirit. The members of the Church have a 'sense of the faith' which is fruit of the presence of the Holy Spirit and his gifts, especially the gift of wisdom. As a result the Church as a whole cannot err in matters of belief. This characteristic of the Church is shown in the *sensus fidei* of the whole people, when 'from the bishops to the last of the faithful' they manifest a universal consent in matters of faith and morals. [11]

Pope Pius XII used the 'sense of the faith' in finding the foundation for defining the dogma of the Assumption. In 1946 he made an official enquiry of all the bishops of the Church asking whether the Assumption of our Lady could be defined and whether they along with their clergy and people desired the definition. The Pope was not asking them for their opinion as private theologians but rather as successors of the Apostles and witnesses of the faith throughout the whole Church. The answer to both questions was an almost unanimous yes. The Pope concluded, 'This common consent is of itself an absolutely certain proof, which admits of no error, that the privilege in question is a truth revealed by God and one contained in that divine deposit which Christ entrusted to his spouse to be faithfully guarded and infallibly proclaimed.' [12]

HARMONY OF PRIVILEGES

The Teaching Authority of the Church has confirmed what the

sensus fidei of the People of God had recognised: that the Assumption of our Lady is implicitly included among the privileges granted by God to Mary on account of her being Mother of God. A privilege is a special provision made for a case that is not adequately resolved in general law. Mary's vocation to be Mother of the Word Incarnate is altogether unique and is surrounded by privileges that accompany it. These privileges are more than mere circumstances. They affect Mary in her inmost being: her fulness of grace, the Incarnation of the Word in her womb, her perpetual virginity, her own conception preserved free from any stain of original sin. By an eternal plan, God grants all these and more to his daughter on whom he looks with unique favour.

The privileges are in harmony with one another and with Mary's exalted role as Mother of God. God's liberality is on a par with his intention not to leave Mary without anything that would take from her dignity or from the veneration that all should show her. It is from here that the believer's love for Mary, which, however strong and lively, is but a pale participation of God's own love for her, leads him to realise that God has in fact crowned the other privileges with a further privilege of comparable magnitude: her Assumption, body and soul, into heaven at the end of her earthly life. We cannot think it to be otherwise. As Saint Robert Bellarmine says, 'our mind revolts at the thought that our Lady's flesh should return to dust'.

THE HOLY SPIRIT MOVES

Such a growth in insight into the deposit of faith is not a chance outcome of philosophical trends. It finds its cause and mover in the Holy Spirit, the Spirit of Truth who proceeds from the Truth and leads to the truth. It was the Holy Spirit who poured the love of the Mother of God into the hearts of generations of believers leading them to see this revealed truth in ever clearer light. The Consoler is active not only in the souls of all the faithful, whether hierarchy or laity, but also he is the mover of the external events that prepared the way for the solemn definition. He is undoubtedly behind the petitions and requests for a definition that came to the Holy See. His hand can also be seen in the crusades of prayer that were set on foot for that intention as well as the active study of the question by eminent theologians and university faculties. All of these external occurences made it more clear that the Assumption of our Lady was contained in the deposit of faith entrusted to the Church. An overwhelming wind was generated from what began as a gentle whisper.

THE EARLIEST TESTIMONIES

The truth that Mary is Mother of God was vindicated at the Council of Ephesus in 431 AD against the attack made on it by Nestorius. There was great rejoicing among the people of the city and the Council Fathers were carried to their lodgings by torchlight procession. It was only a few years before that, in 403, that Saint Epiphanius died, to whom we are indebted for the first extant literary testimony as to how our Lady's life on earth ended. He tells us that in his time no one tradition outweighed another on the question, but that he himself inclined to that which held her departure to be glorious. It is not too surprising that in those early centuries of the faith the tradition on the Assumption would be slow in developing. Many more central truths of the Faith were constantly under attack from heresy and it was these that occupied the minds and thoughts of believers. Besides, God works in an orderly fashion. First the explicit truths — like Mary's being Mother of God — needed to become peacefully established. Then further riches could be manifested.

The fifth century saw a growth in writings with a definite tone of Assumption about them. They all agree that our Lady's body never suffered the corruption of the grave, but still only a few explicitly state that she had a glorious resurrection and anticipated glory in heaven. The most famous of these writings are the *Transitus Mariae,* wrongly attributed for a long time to the pen of Saint Melitus of Sardis and the *Liber Dormitionis* (The Account of the Falling Asleep), wrongly attributed to Saint John the Apostle. These accounts can be taken as a certain testimony of the faith of the people. Some authorities think that they reflect a basis for belief, a tradition, that goes back to the Apostles. Others think it more likely that they are a result of a deep meditation in faith and love on the mysteries of Mary's divine maternity and her perpetual virginity. Whichever is the case, the Church does not draw its dogmas from tenuous literary traditions but is glad to find them supporting her teaching.

The Church manifests her faith in her prayer. *Lex orandi, lex credendi* is a well-known phrase which reflects the intimate connection there is between the Church's faith and its liturgy. The earliest evidence of a feast of the Dormition of Mary relates to the middle of the sixth century. The content of the feast underwent development. First the Passing of Mary was commemorated. Then this feast began to alternate with a feast of the Assumption itself. In the seventh century it had spread both in the East and in the West. By the eight century it became fixed on 15 August and was celebrated in Rome with the same dogmatic content which it has today. The liturgical books of the time testify to the doctrinal basis of the feast: when Mary left this world to go to heaven, what befell her chaste body was consistent with her dignity as Mother of God and with her other privileges. The prayers of the liturgy speak of the impenetrable mystery of the Assumption, unique among men. In Eastern liturgies reference is made to the special links that exist between this privilege and that of Mary's perpetual virginity. Lest anyone think, however, that the dogma of the Assumption made progress on a wave of popular devotion alone, God allowed it to pass through a period of feeble support from a certain section of a great theological advance.

THE HESITATION

After the Dark Ages, learning in Europe took on a new vigour through the schools which grew up around the great cathedrals and monasteries. This intellectual revival produced 'scholastic theology', the theology of the schools. Powerfully blending faith and reason, it laid its foundations squarely on what was contained explicitly in Sacred Scripture and Sacred Tradition. The Bible and the Fathers of the Church were the 'authorities' which carried weight in theological elaborations. The whole of divine Revelation was the theologians' field and they were loath to deal with subjects which were not explicitly mentioned in the 'authorities'. Often the Assumption of Mary was treated with a prudent silence. It was unfortunate that the Scholastics were not as familiar with the Greek Fathers as they were with the Fathers of the West. Had this been the case they could have found many elements in the Greek tradition that they could have used, especially in the connection the Greeks made between our

Lady's virginity and her Assumption.

There were notable exceptions to this trend, however. One author, purporting to be Saint Augustine, anticipated a method in theology that would later become a standard tool. He introduced the argument of suitability in relation to the Assumption. The argument, which is related to the harmony between the mysteries, runs thus: It was fitting that God should do some particular thing, for example, bring Mary, his Mother, body and soul to heaven at the end of her earthly life. He could do it. Therefore, he did in fact do it. Mary was assumed into heaven body and soul. This argument which is very fruitfully applied in many areas of theology is neatly summed up in Latin as *Decuit. Potuit. Ergo fecit.* The casual link in the passage from possibility to the fact is to be found in this case in Christ's filial love for his Mother which led him to do what it was fitting that he should. Mary's dignity as Mother of God and her consequent eminent holiness, along with the close union of Mother and Son, more than indicate the fittingness of the Assumption.

Theologians do not make the faith; they state it and draw out its consequences in a rigorous fashion. The argument of fittingness was to prove a great help to theology in grappling with those truths which are not so explicitly revealed in Scripture and the Fathers. From the twelfth century onwards, this theological approach carried the day in relation to the Assumption of Mary.

PREACHING ON THE FEAST

Meanwhile the liturgical feast of the Assumption was constantly being celebrated more widely and more enthusiastically. Bishops and preachers authorised by them took it upon themselves to explain clearly and eloquently to the faithful the mystery being celebrated. In their preaching they brought out the intimate connection between the Assumption and the other revealed mysteries. They developed and put forth those reasonings that have since become the classic theological supports for the dogma. Even though the Assumption is not explicitly mentioned in the Bible, they often allowed themselves a broad margin of freedom in applying words and events from Scripture to the mystery.

Our Lady is often compared to the ark of the covenant, which was made of incorruptible wood and placed in God's temple. The ark is an image of Mary's chaste body, preserved from all corruption of the tomb and brought to great glory in heaven. [13]

Another Old Testament image of Mary assumed into heaven is taken from Psalm 44. Mary is seen as the queen triumphantly entering the royal court and sitting with honour at the Redeemer King's right. [14]

The preaching of those who have received, along with the right of succession in the episcopate, the sure charism of truth [15] is another of the ways in which growth in insight into the mysteries takes place. Like the theologians, the preachers do not generate the faith. They explain more lucidly what is already accepted by the faithful.

THE DEFINITION

Throughout many generations, the Church, actively and infallibly directed by the Holy Spirit, had manifested its belief in Mary's Assumption in many ways. Pope Pius XII deemed it was the moment preordained in the plan of Divine Providence to solemnly proclaim this extraordinary privilege of the Virgin Mary. He had received an almost unanimous petition from the bishops of the world that the dogma be defined. He had seen that the truth was founded on Scripture, that it was deeply imbedded in the minds of the faithful, that it had received the approval of liturgical worship from earliest times, that it was perfectly in keeping with the rest of revealed truth and had been lucidly developed and explained by the studies of the theologians. Now, with the assistance of the Holy Spirit promised to him in the person of Saint Peter, in an absolute decision as supreme pastor and teacher of all the faithful he proclaimed the dogma of the Assumption.

Solemn definitions are easily recognisable. Their wording leaves no doubt as to their nature. The solemn definition of the Assumption begins with a preamble: 'Wherefore, having directed humble and repeated prayers to God, and having invoked the light of the Spirit of Truth, to the glory of Almighty God, who has bestowed his special bounty on the Virgin Mary, for the honour of his Son, the Immortal King of Ages and Victor over sin and death, for the greater glory of his august Mother and for the exultation of the whole Church . . .' . Then comes the actual definition itself:

By the authority of our Lord Jesus Christ, of the Blessed Apostles Peter and Paul, and by our own, We proclaim, declare and define it to be a dogma revealed by God that the Immaculate Mother of God, Mary every Virgin, when the course of her earthly life was finished, was taken up body and soul into the glory of Heaven. [16]

The titles given to our Lady in the definition, namely, 'Immaculate', 'Mother of God', and 'ever Virgin' are used by the Pope to specify the person to whom the definition refers. It is not implied that these other privileges explain the privilege of the Assumption. It is indeed extremely fitting that the Assumption should crown Mary's other singular graces, but it is a dogma of faith because it was revealed by God. Nevertheless, a consideration however brief of the theological arguments for the Assumption is very worthwhile.

ASSUMPTION AND DIVINE MOTHERHOOD

The most fundamental truth about Mary is that she is Mother of God, chosen for that purpose by an eternal decree of God the Father. Scripture bears out the close unity that there is between the lives of Jesus and Mary. We see her as sharing in God's plan for the salvation of the world brought about by Christ. 'Hence it seems practically impossible to contemplate her who conceived Christ, brought him forth and nourished him with her milk, held him in her arms and embraced him, as separated in body from him, though not in soul, after her life on earth was over'. [17] It was Christ who as God had established the fourth commandment of honouring parents and who as man pleased God his Father by his reverence. [18] He could hardly not honour his mother. And since he could give her such honour as she now has by assuming her body and soul to heaven, the fittingness of the Assumption is so extreme that we must believe that he actually did so.

Pope John Paul II puts it this way:

With what new truth these words resound, which Mary on that day spoke during her visit to Elizabeth: 'My spirit rejoices in God my saviour . . . the Almighty has done great things for me' (Lk 1:47, 49).

Indeed he has done great things to her right from the beginning of her life — from the moment of her conception in the womb of her mother, Anne, when, having chosen her as the mother of his own Son, he freed her from the yoke of the heritage of original sin. And further, during the years of her youth when he called her totally to himself, to his own service, as the bride in the Canticle of Canticles. And then, through the Annunciation, at Nazareth, and through the night of Beth-

lehem, and through the thirty years of the hidden life of Nazareth. And then later, through the experiences of the years of the
teaching-mission of her Son Christ, and the horrible sufferings
of his cross, and the dawn of the resurrection . . .

Truly 'the Almighty has done great things for me, and holy
is his name' (Lk 1:49).

In this instant [the Assumption], the last act of the earthly
dimension is fulfilled. It is an act which is at the same time the
first act of the eternal dimension. In the womb of eternity. [19]

The Christian soul, moreover, finds it repugnant to think that
the body of her from whom the life-giving body and blood of
Christ was totally formed — the Holy Spirit made no material
contribution to the body of Christ — should be subject to the
decay of the grave.

ASSUMPTION AND IMMACULATE CONCEPTION

In view of the merits of Christ, Mary was in the first instant of
her conception preserved from all stain of original sin. This is the
dogma of the Immaculate Conception which was solemnly defined
by Pope Pius IX in 1854, almost a century before the definition of
the Assumption. The two privileges are closely connected and the
definition of the Immaculate Conception prepared the way for the
later definition.

Death entered the world through orginal sin which stains all
men who are conceived through human generation. By his own
death on the Cross, Christ fully overcame sin and death and he
communicates his victory to all who are reborn in his likeness
through the sacrament of Baptism. Yet, by general law, on account of once having had original sin, a person who is saved is not
granted the full effect of Christ's victory until the end of time.
Therefore all men die and their bodies decay.

God willed that Mary should be granted the singular privilege of
being preserved from contracting the stain of original sin in the
moment she was conceived. As a result she was not bound by the
general law of remaining in the corruption of the tomb. Neither
did she have to wait until the end of time for the redemption of
her body, but was assumed body and soul as soon as her earthly
life ended.

Pope John Paul II brings out the relationship of both mysteries
in his teaching. 'It was necessary that she, in whom dwelt the Son
of God as author of the victory over sin and death, would also be

the first to live in God, free from sin and the corruption of the grave: from sin, through her Immaculate Conception; from the corruption of the grave, through the Assumption.' [20]

ASSUMPTION AND VIRGINITY

Mary's divine Motherhood is accompanied by perpetual virginity — before, during and after the birth of Christ. The early Christians — especially in the East — had a deep appreciation of the meaning of virginity. They saw it as much more than just physical integrity. It was completeness of dedication to God, in soul first, but also in body. The bodily integrity faithfully reflects the soul's complete and undamaged commitment to God. During our Lady's lifetime on earth God wished to preserve by miraculous supernatural intervention the bodily expression of her singularly wholehearted love for him. Would he not by a similar supernatural initiative preserve her whole body from corruption in sign of her special holiness, as in fact he did in the Assumption?

ASSUMPTION AND FULNESS OF GRACE

Grace is the life of God shared by our soul. It is often called 'the seed of glory', for when we die it flowers into the vision of God which will make us eternally happy. The ultimate effect of grace is the glorification of the body when the dead rise again. 'Hail, full of grace' [21] is how the Angel greeted Mary. The heavenly messenger celebrates the fulness of all the bountiful gift of God in her. Her grace ranges from the initial grace of the Immaculate Conception to culminate in her final glorification. Mary receives grace in plenitude according to the different stages of her life. The final grace of our Lady in heaven would not be present in its fulness if it did not reach its ultimate effect, the glorification of her body.

We can add also that Mary's grace is special. By it she is assimilated spiritually to Christ as much as he to her physically. The development of Christ's life as regards the effects of grace in his human soul is the immediate glorification of his body. We can expect then that in a like manner Mary's glorification in body and soul will also be immediate.

In his Angelus message of 15 August 1982, Pope John Paul II said: 'Today we pronounce the words "full of grace" as we recall the Assumption of Mary. The fulness of grace which Mary enjoyed from the first instant of her conception, in consideration of the merits of Christ, confirmed her assumption in body and soul.

'The Assumption signifies a definitive union with God — Father-Son-Holy Spirit. Grace leads to this union and its gradual realization during man's earthly life. It is definitively realised in heaven.' [22]

ASSUMPTION: TYPE OF THE CHURCH

The Second Vatican Council teaches that Mary is a type of the Church. In other words, she is a foreshadow of what the Church will one day be in fulness. While she was living on this earth, she was the model of faith, hope, love and holiness to which the pilgrim Church and its members aspire. Now assumed body and soul into heaven, she is the image and beginning of the Church as it is to be perfected in the world to come. [23] The Church will never die a material death before it reaches its final perfection in heaven. Mary assumed into heaven without dying is thus the perfect type of the Church.

'She is that great sign which, according to the words of Saint John in the Apocalypse appeared in the heavens (cf Rev 12:1). This sign is at the present time closely connected with the earth. It is first of all the sign of the struggle "with the dragon" (cf Rev 12:4), and in this struggle we read again the whole story of the Church on earth: the struggle against Satan, the struggle against the forces of darkness, which never cease to attack the Kingdom of God.

'This is at the same time, the sign of the definitive victory. In the mystery of her Assumption, Mary is the sign of this definitive victory, of which the author of the Apocalypse speaks: "Now the salvation and the power and the kingdom of our God and the authority of his Christ have come (Rev 12:10)".' [24]

ASSUMPTION AND THE NEW EVE

As early as the second century, Fathers of the Church began to speak of Mary as the new Eve. Christ is the new Adam with whom she is most closely associated in giving life to the world through his victory over sin and death on the Cross. Saint Paul sees Christ's victory to be total when the body rises again. 'Then when this mortal nature wears its immortality, the saying of Scripture will come true "Death is swallowed up in victory." ' [25]

Mary's intimate union and participation in the mystery of the Incarnation and Redemption imply a full union and participation in Christ's victory. The resurrection is an essential part of the victory. Mary's share in it would not be complete unless she received anticipated glory. Christ rose from the dead and ascended into heaven. Mary was assumed body and soul into heaven.

'It was necessary that she, who was the Mother of the Risen Christ, would be the first among men to participate in the full power of his resurrection.' [26]

Mind and will interact in such a complex fashion that it often occurs that behaviour is more effectively influenced for the better by preaching of the great speculative truths than by the most earnest practical exhortations. By revealing the Assumption of Mary into heaven to be contained in the deposit of faith, God has given the Church and each of us its members a strong stimulus to strive towards that holiness in mind and body which Mary assumed into heaven puts before us. A piety devoid of doctrine would run the risk of subsiding into sentimentality. Doctrine without piety would be lifeless. A strong Marian piety nourished by the loving contemplation of the mysteries of Mary's life has been the providential means whereby the Church has grown in insight into the more hidden contents of revealed truth. It is up to each of us to keep the path of progress open for further advance through a confident love for Mary, our Mother assumed body and soul into heaven.

Notes

NOTE to Adams, *On being Catholics for Right Reasons*

1. '.. I was once, five or six years ago, taken by some friends to have dinner with Mary McCarthy and her husband, Mr Broadwater. (She just wrote that book, *A Charmed Life*.) She departed the Church at the age of 15 and is a Big Intellectual. We went at eight and at one, I hadn't opened my mouth once, there being nothing for me in such company to say. The people who took me were Robert Lowell and his now wife, Elizabeth Hardwick. Having me there was like having a dog present who had been trained to say a few words but overcome with inadequacy had forgotten them. Well, toward morning the conversation turned on the Eucharist, which I, being the Catholic, was obviously supposed to defend. Mrs Broadwater said when she was a child and received the Host, she thought of it as the Holy Ghost. He being the "most port-

able" person of the Trinity; now she thought of it as a symbol and implied that it was a pretty good one. I then said, in a very shaky voice, "Well, if it's a symbol, to hell with it." That was all the defense I was capable of but I realize now that this is all I will ever be able to say about it, outside of a story, except that it is the center of existence for me; all the rest of life is expendable. ... ': letter to 'A.', 16 December 1955 in Flannery O'Connor, *The Habit of Being*: Letters edited and with an introduction by Sally Fitzgerald, New York 1980, pp. 124-125.

NOTES to Connolly, *The Blessed Eucharist*

1. While this article deals expressly with the sacramental aspect of the Eucharist it is important to remember that the Eucharist is also a sacrifice; in fact, in the words of Pope John Paul II 'The Eucharist is above all else a sacrifice . . . This sacrificial value is expressed . . . in every celebration by the words with which the priest concludes the presentation of the gifts, asking the faithful to pray "that my sacrifice and yours may be acceptable to God, the almighty Father." These words are binding, since they express the character of the entire Eucharistic liturgy and the fullness of its divine and ecclesial content' *(The Holy Eucharist*, n. 9, 24 February 1980, (CTS translation).

2. Vatican II, *Decree on the Life and Ministry of Priests*, no. 5.

3. St. Justin Martyr, *First Apology*, Chap. 66.

4. J. Escrivá de Balaguer, *Christ is passing by* (Dublin 1982), no. 84.

5. Pope Paul VI, Enc. *The Mystery of faith* (C.T.S.), no. 38.

6. Cf. *idem*, nos. 34-38.   7. *Idem*, no. 39.

8. Francis Clark, A *'new theology' of the Real Presence*, CTS, Do 396, no. 20.   9. St. Ignatius of Antioch, *Ep. to the Smyrnaeans VII*.

10. Cf Paul VI, *The Mystery of faith*, nos. 10-11.

11. Declaration of faith of Berengarius of Tours, Dz. 700 (355).

12. Council of Trent in *The Catholic Church teaches*, n.719.

13. Zwingli, as quoted in Smith, *The Teaching of the Catholic Church*, p. 842, Dz 860 (465).   14. Council of Lyons II.

16. St Irenaeus of Lyons, *Adv. Haer*, IV, 18, 4.   17. *Hom. 82 in Matt*, n. 4.

18. *Idem*.   19. *Hom 46 in Joann*.   20. *First Apology*, chap. 66.

21. *Decree on the Church*, n. 7.

22. *Summa theologica*, III, 75, I c.

23. Fulton Sheen, *Life of Christ*, p. 155.

24. Smith, *op. cit.*, p 847.

25. Victor Galeone, 'The Real Presence, fact or fantasy?' in *Pastoral and Homiletic Review*, Aug/Sept., 1978, pp. 12-13.

26. St Ambrose, *De Myster*, 9.

27. Instruction on Communion under both species in *Vatican II on Liturgy*, ed. Flannery (Dublin 1968), p. 207.

28. *General Instruction on Roman Missal*, no. 242.

29. *Idem*, no. 240.   30. *Idem*, no. 241.   31. *Idem*.

32. Instruction on distribution of Holy Communion in *Vatican II on Liturgy*, ed. Flannery, p. 153.

33. Instruction on distribution of Holy Communion in particular circumstances, in *Vatican II*, ed. Flannery, p. 231.

34. Council of Trent, Dz 1654 (886).   35. *Idem,* Dz 1657 (889).

36. J. Escrivá de Balaguer, *op. cit.,* no. 156.

37. E. Boylan, *This tremendous lover,* pp. 162-3.

38. Council of Trent, Dz 1656 (888).

39. St Augustine, *Ennar. in Ps.* 98:9.   40. *Catechism of Pius V*, p. 221.

41. St Ambrose, *De Sacrm.* IV, 4, 14.

42. Council of Florence, Dz 1322 (698).

43. Council of Florence, Dz 1322 (698).

44. Cf. Eph 20:2.   45. *Adv. Haer,* IV, 18, 5.

46. Cf. *Position Papers,* No. 51, Dublin, Dublin, March 1978.

47. J. Escrivá de Balaguer, *The Way* (Dublin 1981) n. 536.

48. Cf. *Position Papers,* No. 25, January 1976.

49. Cf. Flannery (ed.), *op. cit.*

50. Cf. Pope Pius XII, Apost. Const. *Christus Dominus,* 6 January 1953.

51. *Serm* 84, 3.   52. Vatican II, *Constitution on the Liturgy,* no. 47.

NOTES to Rodriguez, *The Primacy of the Pope*

1. W. Pannenberg in *Una Sancta* 30 (1975) 220-221.

2. *Authority in the Church. A statement on the question of authority, its nature, exercise and implication.* Agreed by the Anglican-Roman Catholic International Commission, Venice 1976. London, CTS/SPCK, 1977, n. 23.   3. *Decree on ecumenism,* no. 11.

4. DS 3302 (1954). The emphases are in the original, AAS 28 (1895/96) 710. The Pope applies the principle to the particular case of the unity of the Church which he is dealing with in his encyclical letter.

5. *Decree on ecumenism,* no. 4.

6. Paul VI, *Address to Vatican Council II,* 14 Sept 1964, AAS 56 (1964) 807.

7. A. del Portillo, *Faithful and laity in the Church,* Shannon 1976, p. 19.

8. *Ibidem,* p. 22.

9. St Pius X, Enc. *Vehementer,* 11 Feb 1906, AAS 39 (1906) 8.

10. DS 1776 (966), 3051 (1821).   11. Decree *on the Church,* no. 19.

12. *Ibidem,* no. 20.   13. *Ibidem,* no. 18.   14. *Ibidem,* no. 20.

15. Conc. of Trent, Sess 23, c. 6, DS 1776 (966).

16. *Decree on the Church,* no. 20.   17. *Ibidem,* no. 21 and 28.

18. *Ibidem,* no. 18.   19. DS 1307 (694).   20. DS 3051 (1921).

21. *Decree on the Church,* no. 18.   22. DS 3055 (1823).

23. DS 3053 (1822).   24. DS 3054 (1822).

25. Cf for example L. Bouyer, *L'Eglise de Dieu, Corps de Christ, et Temple de l'Esprit,* Paris 1970., pp. 460-468. 'The evangelists were convinced that the function of Peter in the early Church was in no way the result of an outstanding personality, but of a *formal disposition of Christ* and therefore, of a charism corresponding to a particular situation' (p. 462).

26. DS 3058 (1825).   27. Cf Note 12 above.

28. D 112 and DS 3056 (1824).

29. St Irenaeus, *Adversus Haereses*, III, 3, 2.

30. DS 3064 (1831).   31. DS 3064 (1831).

32. Vatican Council I, the theologians tell us, made this affirmation in a positive, not an exclusive way, for the episcopal college, with the Pope at its head, also has full and supreme power in the Church (cf *Decree on the Church*, no. 22) and in this sense has a power equal to the Pope's power.   33. DS 3060 (1827).

34. The power of the Pope is not to be thought of as standing in the way of the power of the bishops, each in his own diocese; cf. DS 3061 (1827).

35. Paul VI, *Address* 29 March 1967.   36. *Decree on the Church*, no. 24.

37. St Leo the Great, *Sermon III on the Nativity*.   38. DS 3060 (1827).

39. For this reason Vatican II affirmed the right of the Pope to communicate freely with the bishops and faithful of the whole Church, cf. DS 3062 (1929).

40. Cardinal Seper, *Introductory address to the Synod of Bishops* 1969.

41. DS 3063 (1830).

42. M. Schmaus, *Teologica Dogmatica, IV: La Iglesia*. Madrid 1960, p. 462.

43. G. Philips, *L'Eglise et son mystere au IIe Concile du Vatican*, Paris 1967, 297.

44. J. Ratzinger, *Das neue Volk Gottes*, Dusseldorf 1969, p. 169.

45. Paul VI, *Address*, 27 Oct. 1969, AAS 61 (1969), 728.

46. J. Escrivá de Balaguer, 1965.   47. *Idem*, 1943.   48. Paul VI, *o.c.*

49. DS 3065-3073/1832-1840. The author refers to the first part of this essay which was first published in English in *Position Papers*, no. 85, Dublin, January 1981 and later in *Osservatore Romano* (English edition), 14 September 1981.

50. In the first draft of this scheme the title was 'The infallibility of the Roman Pontiff'. It was changed to the final title in order to stress what I indicate: it is not the person who is infallible but his personal magisterium. See P. Rodriguez *'Infallibilis?* St Thomas' reply' in *Scripta Theologica* 7 (1975), pp 120-121.   51. DS 3065/1832.

52. Council of Trent, sess. 5, can. 2, n. 9. 'D. de reform.'

53. *Lumen Gentium* 25.   54. Ibid.   55. DS 3051/1821.

56. *Lumen Gentium* 25.   57. Ibid.

58. See *L'infallibilite de l'Eglise* (Chevetogne, 1966).

59. I refer to reports etc. re the Holy See's decision to withdraw Professor Hans Küng's *missio canonica* to teach Catholic theology. Küng in his *Unfehlbar. Eine Anfrage (Einsiedeln* 1970) parted company with Catholic doctrine on the infallibility of the Church. See, e.g. the documentation of this affair issued by the German conference of bishops: *Le Dossier Küng Faits et Documents* (Paris 1980).

60. Declaration *Mysterium Ecclesiae* (S. Cong. for Doctrine of the Faith), 24 June 1973, n. II.

61. 'No one is good but God alone' (Mk 10:18); but 'God is true' (Rom 3:4); 'God is not man that he should lie' (Num 23:19).

62. See P. Rodriguez, *Iglesia y Ecumenismo* (Madrid 1979), chap. II.

63. DS 3070/1836.   64. Const. *Dei Verbum*, 10.   65. See 1 Cor 13:8-12.
66. This is the way the fourth Lateran Council put it in 1215: see DS 806/ 432.   67. See council texts in Mansi, vol. 52, col 1213.
68. DS 3070/1836.   69. Mansi, vol. 53, col 268-269.   70. DS 3074/1089.
71. See. G. Redondo, *La Iglesia en el Mundo Contemporaneo, I: De Pio VI a Pio IX* (Pamplona 1979) pp. 276-278.
72. Mansi, vol. 53, col. 313.   73. *Summa Theologica* 2-2, q.1, a.9.
74. Article 3 of the question cited from the *Summa* covers this subject. See DS 1534/1802.
75. Cf. G. Thils, 'L'infallibilite de l'Eglise dans la Const. *Pastor Aeternus* du Premier Concile du Vatican', in the book referred to on note 58.
76. The text of the dogmatic definition is to be found in DS 3073/1839. The quoted phrases in what follows are taken from its.
77. Michael Schmaus, *Teologica Dogmatica* IV (Madrid 1960), p. 462.
78. *Lumen Gentium* 25.   79. DS 3073/1839.
80. *Lumen Gentium* 25.   81. DS 3073/1839.
82. This 'has allowed us to grasp better the distinction between the *sensus Ecclesiae* (to which the Pope, as an organ of Tradition must always relate) and the *consensus Ecclesiae* (on which he is not dependent).
83. *Lumen Gentium* 25.   84. Ibid.   85. Ibid.   86. Ibid.   87. Ibid.
88. Ibid. This whole subject has been studied at length in J. Sancho, *Infalibilidad del Pueblo de Dios* (Pamplona 1959).
89. Paul VI, *Address*, 27 October 1969 in AAS 61), p. 728.
90. J. Escrivá de Balaguer, Rome, 1965.   91. Ibem, Madrid, 1943.
92. Paul VI, Address to Vatican Council II, 14 September 1964 in AAS 56 (1964), p. 812.   93. Text in *Ecclesia* 40 (1980), p. 91.

NOTES to Sweeney, *On the Assumption of our Lady*

1. Pius XII, *Apostolic Constitution Munificentissimus Deus* (MD) 46, 1 November 1950. Paragraph numbers are from the Irish Messenger Office edition.   2. Second Vatican Council, *Dogmatic Constitution on Divine Revelation Dei Verbum* (DV) 4 and 7. Paragraph numbers are from the Dominican Publications, Dublin edition.
3. MD 47, 48, 49.   4. DV 10.   5. DV 8.   6. DV 8.   7. DV 8.
8. Saint Thomas Acquinas, *Super Evangelium S. Ioannis Lectura* c. 5, lect. 6: 'Per ardorem caritatis datur cognitio veritatis.'
9. John Paul II, Homily at Castlegandolfo, 15 August 1980 in John Paul II, *This is your Mother*, ed. Seamus O'Byrne (Athlone 1981), p. 155.
10. Heb. 11:1.   11. Second Vatican Council, *Dogmatic Constitution on the Church Lumen Gentium* (LG) 12.   12. MD 10.   13. Ps 131:8.
14. Ps 44:10; 14-16.   15. DV 8.   16. MD 53.   17. MD 45.
18. See Heb 5:7.   19. John Paul II, Homily at Castlegandolfo, 15 August 1979.   20. See (19) above.   21. Lk 1:28.   22. John Paul II, Angelus Message, 15 August 1982.   23. See LG 63, 65, 68.
24. John Paul II, Homily at Castlegandolfo, 15 August 1982.   25. 1 Cor 15:24.   26. John Paul II, Homily at Castlegandolfo, 15 August 1982.